T0292799

**BOCCONI
UNIVERSITY
PRESS**

Marco Bardazzi

SILICON EUROPE

The Great Adventure of the Global Chip Industry and an Italian-French Company that Makes the World Go Round

Foreword by **Nicolas Dufourcq** and **Maurizio Tamagnini**

Original Title: *Silicon Europe. La grande avventura della microelettronica e di un'azienda italofrancese che fa girare il mondo*
© 2022 STMicroelectronics
First edition in Italian published by BUR Rizzoli / Mondadori Libri S.p.A.

Translation: Jill Connelly
Cover: Cristina Bernasconi, Milan
Photo credit: © STMicroelectronics
Typesetting: Laura Panigara, Cesano Boscone (MI)

English edition © 2023 Egea S.p.A. published in agreement with BEA MEDIA COMPANY S.r.l.

EGEA S.p.A.
Via Salasco, 5 - 20136 Milano
Tel. 02/5836.5751 – Fax 02/5836.5753
egea.edizioni@unibocconi.it – www.egeaeditore.it

First edition: December 2023

ISBN Domestic Edition	979-12-80623-23-2
ISBN Digital Domestic Edition	978-88-238-8710-7
ISBN International Edition	979-12-81627-02-4
ISBN Digital International Edition	979-12-81627-03-1

Table of Contents

Foreword.
A Story of Visionaries

by *Nicolas Dufourcq*[*] and *Maurizio Tamagnini*[**]

When we look at what STMicroelectronics is today, it's hard to fully grasp how long and challenging the path was that led to its current size and the prominent role it plays in the world of semiconductors. This book tries to tell the story of a world leader with a French-Italian heart and brain. We are pleased that now the general public can learn about ST's long history, dating back to the 1950s and 1960s, and some of its great managers and scientists.

Silicon Europe is the demonstration that it is possible to create a large European high-tech leader, with huge investments in research and sizeable investments in factories in Europe, in one of the most capital-intensive, cyclical, and competitive industries.

The main actor in this captivating tale is ST: a corporation that was pictured as an albatross by its first CEO, Pasquale Pistorio, when nearly no one believed it had a future. "It's been scientifically proven that the albatross cannot fly, but it doesn't know that, so it keeps on flying. At ST, we did the same."

Silicon Europe is the story of high-profile alliances forged with major international groups, partnerships that helped ST grow in size and thrive, enabling it to co-develop cutting-edge products with determination and a clear vision; empowering it to become first sustainable, and then profitable. And all this explains why today ST has revenues

---

[*] Chairman of the STMicroelectronics Supervisory Board.
[**] Vice Chairman of the STMicroelectronics Supervisory Board.

of over $17 billion and more than 200,000 small, medium and large customers.

Silicon Europe is the story of ST's stability. In fact, in 35 years, the company has had only three CEOs: Pasquale Pistorio, Carlo Bozotti, and now Jean-Marc Chery. Jean-Marc is leading, with tremendous foresight and pragmatism, one of the few European companies that has risen to be among the ten largest semiconductor manufacturers in the world.

Silicon Europe tells frames of the history of the French and Italian economies over the past 60 years. There are names that made their mark in Italian industry, such as Adriano Olivetti and Virgilio Floriani, or left their mark in the US and in Europe, the likes of Pasquale Pistorio, Bruno Murari, Aldo Romano, and Federico Faggin. There is France, which has had a world-class school in the field of semiconductors since the 1950s, with scholars and business leaders of international caliber: Pierre Aigrain, Charles Dugas, and Maurice Ponte, followed by Roland Moreno, Jacques Noels, and Alain Gomez.

The book is testament to the fact that deep tech projects require a long time and shareholder stability to flourish. This stability is provided by the governments of two great countries, France and Italy, long-term investors who have always been supportive in critical moments. Large risky projects need time to produce results. And they need managers with a vision spanning decades, who forge ahead with daring investments which might sometimes be considered impossible. Like the huge gambles in products and sectors that didn't yet exist, and new factories in far-away regions, like the first plant in Singapore in 1968, and similar initiatives that followed in Morocco, Malaysia, and China.

Silicon Europe is the story of how ethics and sustainability are inborn in companies led by forward-looking leaders. In the early 1990s, ST had already established sustainability as one of its key principles in all its meeting rooms around the world.

Silicon Europe is a showcase of ambitious goals and dreams. Companies start small, but they must increase in size. Way back in 1983, when the fragile little SGS had just turned a small profit, Pistorio shared his vision with his managers: i) to become one of the top ten global semiconductor manufacturers, ii) to be better than industry average in profitability, and iii) to be recognized as a leader in sustainability.

And finally, *Silicon Europe* gives us definitive evidence that it is possible to combine the strategic interests of two governments (France and Italy) and the rules of the market, through modern, stable, long-standing governance. For more or less 30 years now, ST has been successfully combining shareholder participation of two countries, and listing on three stock exchanges (Milan, Paris and New York), with a 67 percent public float and a market capitalization in excess of $40 billion. An example of governance that should serve as an example to build more European corporate champions.

The hope is that the new generation of young people – Italian, French, and European – will draw inspiration from *Silicon Europe*, and give rise to a new Renaissance in European electronics. Just like the albatross does when it flies, with a touch of rational scientific folly.

1   Explosions of Ink

The printers from Oregon

There were six of them, and they booked the hotel for a week.

They were arriving from all over: their headquarters in Corvallis, Oregon, and Silicon Valley, and sales offices in Europe. They all converged in Milan. A clear sign that something was up, something major. A big company didn't move a team like that just for a getting-to-know-you session. And the company these six people worked for wasn't just big – it was a global giant.

But now that they were all together in a meeting room in Castelletto, near Cornaredo in the Milanese hinterland, they didn't seem to be in any rush to show their hand. They wanted to see if the people sitting on the other side of the table – a French-Italian team they'd heard very good things about – could actually fix their problem. A technological and industrialization challenge that would take plenty of experience but also a massive dose of creativity. The idea they had in mind was fairly clear, but they knew that making it materialize would not be simple.

At stake was the future of a business still in its infancy, but with phenomenal growth potential: printers for the office and the home. Some of the technical experts in the conference room worked for the research center that had successfully developed the first inkjet printer in 1984, just a few years before. An innovation that came on the scene right when personal computers started taking off, the very same year that IBM launched the PC Junior as a challenger to the Apple II, to which Steve Jobs responded with the Macintosh, presented to the market in a TV ad comparing Apple's rivals to Big Brother in the Orwellian masterpiece, *1984*. That marked the moment when everyone wanted a computer where they lived and worked. And everyone wanted to print, print, print. Nobody knew how to meet this demand better than HP, the giant that Bill Hewlett and David Packard started building in 1938 in a Palo Alto garage, in a valley just outside San Francisco that was home to nothing more than orchards back then. Three more decades would go by before it would be rebranded, thanks to the silicon boom.

Hewlett-Packard broke into the printer market by making huge investments in efforts to develop affordable models that would win over not only large corporate offices, but also families and retail customers. Two teams were racing to develop the printers that HP would market. In Boise, Idaho, the first team was working on laser printer technology. In this segment, Xerox was the main rival, the team to beat. Once the queen of the photocopiers, Xerox had morphed into a printer pioneer back in the 1970s. The famous Xerox Palo Alto Research Center (PARC) was one of the most creative spaces in Silicon Valley. It was here that researchers had developed a laser technology that was a big hit with large companies – but it came with a hefty price tag. So along came HP to challenge the supremacy of Xerox in 1984, debuting the first-ever affordable laser printer: the LaserJet.

While all this was happening, the second HP team back in Corvallis, Oregon, was inventing a new process that opened up a second market: inkjet printing. That same fateful year – 1984 – marked the debut of the groundbreaking ThinkJet, which showed potential, but had many limitations as well, and the costs were still too high. Later generations of printers continued to evolve: PaintJet and QuietJet.[1] But the real breakthrough didn't come until 1987 with the launch of the first DeskJet, which became the company's flagship product. This printer could attain the same resolution as a laser printer: 300 dpi (dots per inch). What's more, it worked with single-load sheets

---

[1] *Hewlett-Packard Journal*, August 1988. https://www.hpl.hp.com/hpjournal/pdfs/IssuePDFs/1988-08.pdf

instead of the bulky, fan-folded continuous paper with perforated edges.[2]

But the challenge to innovate was constant, partly because of global competition that had been unleashed in the sector, and there was one magic word: *disposable*. For HP, the most powerful part of inkjet technology and the quality of the results depended on cheap, disposable cartridges that users could throw away once the ink ran out. This was what made it possible to sell high-performance printers at reasonable prices. And it was also a huge business.

But now, as the 1990s began, with the PC market on fire and blazing hotter than ever, the evolution in printer models came up against an obstacle and had to find a way over it. At Corvallis they were working on production materials, costs, and logistics. But it was becoming increasingly clear that real innovation was linked to printer cartridges and printer heads. What HP needed were new solutions, big production capacity, and boundless flexibility.

This was what brought those six people from HP to the meeting room in Castelletto, in the offices of an Italian-French company with a complicated name – a name that reflected its beleaguered and riveting history: SGS-Thomson (already known back then as ST for short).

An unexpected dinner

The company the Americans went to visit had $1.6 billion in turnover in 1992, and was nearly back in the black after several bleak years. ST operated in various sectors of the electronics industry: power units, nonvolatile memory, microprocessor technologies, and advanced integrated circuits.

ST had been scouting around for new markets and new clients in the US for some time. But it wasn't easy to carve out space in an industry such as semiconductors, which was dominated by American powerhouses such as Intel, Motorola, and Texas Instruments. When

---

[2] See the Printers section of the HP Computer Museum. http://www.hpmuseum.net/exhibit.php?class=5&cat=19

a few years earlier Italy's Società Generale Semiconduttori (SGS, under the IRI-STET Group) and France's Thomson S.A. merged, the new company that was formed could finally go head to head with titans from the US and Asia, such as Toshiba, Samsung, and Hitachi. But translating sales potential into actual business agreements was no mean feat, even if ST had already landed a few solid punches. For example, around the same time, the company's architecture and products had been chosen for the launch of the first digital satellite TV program: DirecTV.

The lucky break that brought HP all the way to Castelletto happened thanks to an unexpected dinner. At that time, Carlo Bozotti, an ST manager who would later become CEO,[3] represented the company in the US. Carlo was in Silicon Valley for a series of meetings scheduled with prospects such as Western Digital, and with established customers such as Seagate. Bozotti recalls:

"One day, our point person for the computer industry in the US asked me if I wanted to go to San Jose with him for a kind of last-minute dinner with some people from HP's purchasing department. There wasn't anything specific on the agenda, but I went anyway.

At dinner, they talked to me about how they needed to implement, industrialize and produce – in huge volumes – a strange process that required very large chips with a few transistors. They didn't give away much, but it was clear that they were talking about something completely different from micro-lithography – which we had been working on back then to produce increasingly thinner and more sophisticated chips. I explained that for both the technology and the production capacity we could explore what they needed. I put it out there: 'We are definitely interested.'"

Now it was up to the technicians gathered in that meeting room to figure out whether there really was room to work together. Interfacing with the HP delegation, there was an ST working group led by Aldo Romano, who was in charge of ST's Dedicated Products Group, and Bruno Murari, director of ST's R&D labs and head of the inventors

---

[3] The formal title for the head of ST is President and Chief Executive Officer.

working on this product category. Two of the world's leading experts in semiconductors, since the early 1960s they had been working at Agrate Brianza and Castelletto, company headquarters in the outskirts of Milan. There was no one better than Romano and Murari to make this particular "American dream" come true.

> "The first day they explained that they wanted to make some sort of power unit which had something to do with printer cartridges, but they didn't give us many details," Murari recalls. "That very evening we worked on an initial proposition and their reaction was: 'Sounds great, but too expensive.' That was when they threw out a word, but we didn't really understand what it was referring to at first: *disposable.* They explained that the product we were talking about was something you would use for a while and then throw away when the ink ran out. That's why it had to be functional and cheap."

For people used to developing circuits that had to last a long time, and resist all sorts of chemical and physical stresses, this was a whole new ball game.

But even more surprising was discovering what the Americans were looking for in Milan. As mutual trust slowly grew, the technical characteristics of what HP needed started to become clearer. It had all started with an accident in a lab some time before. A researcher was fiddling around with a chip with resistors connected to a pulsed power supply when he knocked over his coffee cup (a standard feature in any American lab). The boiling beverage spilled on the chip and turned into little droplets that shot out all over. Seeing the aftereffects of this accident was the inspiration for an idea that in short order materialized as a patent for the inkjet mechanism in printers. But with this came the need to figure out a more sophisticated way to control the droplets of ink.

The ink cartridges that were starting to inundate the global printer market basically contained sponges that absorbed all the ink and then released it through microscopic tubes that worked like capillaries. A resistor heated the ink to 800 degrees Fahrenheit in three microseconds. This created minuscule droplets that then flowed through hundreds of minute openings, a few microns in diameter, until they funneled into a single drop. This drop then shot out onto the printer paper a few centimeters away to create a letter or graphic symbol. It was a sophisticated controlled explosion, an extremely difficult process to accomplish. The secret to making the outcome more precise was to create channels and a circuit where the ink would flow. HP had already mastered this process thanks to its expertise in the complex realm of microfluidics.

Now they wanted to take it one step further. The Americans had come to Europe to sound out an idea: They wanted to put this entire microscopic labyrinth on a silicon chip, carving out tiny pathways that would allow them to contend with the laws of thermodynamics affecting the process. The microfluidic technique had already been developed in US labs. So at this point, it was a matter of inventing a new process and inserting the whole thing in a disposable cartridge. But disposable meant it had to be affordable, despite all the sophisticated technology it would take to produce.

The search for answers took HP from Silicon Valley to Silicon Europe, a district populated by silicon experts with an epicenter lying between Lombardy, Rhône-Alpes, and Provence. Silicon Europe spans an area from Agrate Brianza and the research center in Castelletto (both on the outskirts of Milan) to the factories of the former Thomson in Grenoble, Rousset, and Tours, extending south to the research center and manufacturing plant in Catania (Sicily). There were also production and distribution centers beyond Europe's borders, including a well-established US presence. Would Silicon Europe's researchers be able to tackle this challenge?

"We held several technical meetings," Romano recalls, "and eventually the time came when we had to decide what to tell the Americans. Should we work with them or not? Did we know how to do it or not? I looked at Bruno and asked him: 'Do you feel up to developing this bizarre thing? Do you think you can do it?' As always, he gave me an honest answer: 'I have no idea whatsoever.' That didn't help me much to decide what do to. But he immediately added: 'What I do know is that if there is a team and a company in the world that can actually make this thing, we are that team.'"

A challenge that came from afar

In that very moment, when they decided to accept HP's challenge, a collaboration began that has continued for 30 years. Still today it's the foundation of the technology used to make the cartridges that supply millions and millions of printers all over the world. It took less than three months for Romano and Murari to be ready with the first "basket" of 6-inch silicon slices loaded with 2.5-micron circuits, custom-built for HP. Next, a researcher flew to the US to test them; everything worked fairly well from the start. Then, to perfect the process, an entire team left for Oregon to work alongside HP's printer research unit. Before long, a production line was set up in the SGS-Thomson factory in Carrollton, Texas, and since that first batch, the plant has manufactured several generations of inkjet printer products.[4]

As time went on, the scope of the collaboration expanded to include HP brand protection equipment. "To this day, whoever has an HP printer, when they buy a cartridge, they are buying a product with an ST chip that guarantees quality and prevents cloning," explains Claude Dardanne, who headed the microcontroller unit at ST for many years.[5] "We started to work with HP on this front in 1998 and the partnership continues thanks to the level of security that our chips effectively guarantee for their cartridges."

The HP case is an example of a bond between companies that goes beyond a simple business agreement. Like many other partnerships that emerged in those years, this was a demonstration that Silicon Europe had reached a milestone. Underpinning those microscopic

---

[4] *"ST/HP Dieci anni di successi insieme"* [Ten Years of Success Together], *WorldClass*, internal STMicroelectronics corporate publication, no. 66, February 2003.

[5] Microcontrollers, one of the most important devices in the world of electronics, are one of the main specializations of STMicroelectronics. These electronic circuits integrate the processing power of a microprocessor on a single chip, and many other functions as well. Microcontrollers are specifically used to manufacture control equipment, and are widely found in consumer electronics, in the automotive sector, and in security applications such as chips on bank cards.

circuits carved into silicon and crisscrossed by minuscule streams of ink, there is a decades-long history of Italian and French intuition and innovation that can be traced back to the 1950s.

The trail was blazed by visionary entrepreneurs and managers such as Adriano Olivetti, Virgilio Floriani, and Maurice Ponte as well as academics who pioneered the field of electronics such as Pierre Aigrain, Yves Rocard, Charles Dugas, and Mario Tchou. They had contact with the US Nobel prize winners who invented the transistor, and with the semiconductor culture nurtured in the legendary labs of Fairchild and Intel and in the research centers of Bell Labs, Carnegie Mellon University, Berkeley, and Stanford. There is an entire European micro-electronics school whose axes run through the outskirts of Milan and Paris, at Agrate (SGS) and in Puteaux (CSF, the largest of the companies that merged into Thomson). The Americans and the Asians have nothing on the Europeans in this field.

The confidence of Bruno Murari when he accepted the challenge – "If anyone can do it, we can!" – may seem like bravado, but it was based on a rational awareness of everything that had come before. He knew it was possible to make microcircuits carved into silicon because one of ST's inventions from a few years before was a one-of-a-kind process called BCD (which we'll be talking a lot about). This enabled the company to explore ways to do the thing HP was asking for: control explosions of super-heated ink. And the experience gleaned during the HP project inspired ideas that a short time later led to the creation of another jewel: MEMS. For now, suffice it to say that MEMS are objects based on accelerometers and gyroscopes that make it possible to convey information about movement. If you enjoy playing fitness video games in your living room, or if your cellphone can tell you how many steps you've taken today, this is almost certainly thanks to MEMS.

From printers to smartphones, from cars to space shuttles, we live in a world of semiconductors and chips that are continually evolving. But we are rarely aware of all the creativity and technology hidden inside our little traveling companions, tiny devices that are driving progress in the world. All too often we think that these innovations are "Made in the USA" or built in an Asian foundry. For this reason, it's worthwhile looking back to see just how much of the history of microelectronics has its roots in Europe, and what the prospects are for the future of this industry.

It is a voyage that will take us over the Alps and back again, between France and Italy, in a journey of discovery to the capitals of silicon.

Welcome to Silicon Europe.

2   Crolles: The Home of Silicon

A chip for everyone

Half a century ago they sent man to the moon, today they help us take our kids to school, and tomorrow they'll take us to Mars. In the meantime, semiconductors allow us to do millions of other things that we normally take for granted.

It is hard to find moments in our daily lives that are not linked to digital activity of one kind or another, and all of them are possible thanks to silicon microchips. Even countless analog processes function because they contain electronic components based on semiconductors: power units, audio applications, sound and video systems for TVs, automation devices that make elevators and traffic lights work. A midsize car currently requires anywhere from 1,000 to 3,000 analog and digital chips (and some luxury cars already have as many as 15,000). As the number of electronic devices on the dashboard grows, and as we transition to electric mobility, the average number will soon hit 10,000.

The digital revolution we've been immersed for over 50 years now, in a certain sense, is actually built on sand – that is, on silicon. Silicon is the raw material that has enabled engineers to develop transistors, integrated circuits, microprocessors, and microcontrollers, which eventually became the components of the first personal computers in the 1970s and 1980s. Silicon is what made so much more possible: the software boom, the birth of the Internet, and the launch of huge platforms that support a sizeable chunk of the global economy (Amazon, Google, Microsoft, and all the others).

Our smartphones, which have changed our daily lives, are brimming with silicon semiconductors. These devices have enabled digitalization, which in turn has led to a new way of consuming content, much of which is now detached from its traditional vehicle: music, after deserting vinyl, has abandoned CDs; movies have dropped DVDs; most news doesn't come to us in newspapers or on TV screens anymore. We've entered a phase of constant content streaming, where content vehicles are smartphones and other devices that are mobile or even wearable (watches, eyeglasses – and there are many more wearables on the way). This process is still proliferating rapidly, with microchip producers at the center of all these activities. It's a transformation that's driven by digital, but analog technology is destined to expand too, with the introduction of artificial intelligence in so many of our daily activities.

All the input we humans perceive is analog: sounds, lights, smells, and so on. Digital, in contrast, basically involves transmitting information on just two levels: 0 and 1. The perceptions and the reasoning that happens in our brains is based on analog stimuli. Any attempt to replicate human biology in chips – to attain increasingly sophisticated artificial intelligence – will require combining more semiconductor-based analog hardware with digital. What's more, the advent of Web 3.0 is likely to set off an explosion in demand for augmented reality and virtual reality to navigate future metaverses. The scenarios that may open up will reveal a future where digital and analog electronics work side by side, allowing for deeper interaction between the physical and computerized worlds.[1]

Just as we value electric power during a blackout, we only appreciate the importance of chips when the supply runs out. The global market for semiconductor production and distribution, one of the most complex and extensive in the world, is subject to cyclical crises and instability. But as with many other human activities, this market never experienced anything like the COVID-19 pandemic. The resulting economic slowdown in 2020 prompted hundreds of millions

[1] Semiconductor Research Corporation, "The Decadal Plan for Semiconductors," December 2020. https://www.src.org/about/decadal-plan/

of people to rush to buy appliances and electronics, as they suddenly found themselves forced to work and study from home. Then in 2021-22 came an escalation in orders for everything, impacting every industry, which in turn triggered a shortage of semiconductors. But there was a silver lining: everyone, even nonexperts, came to realize just how vital these components truly are in modern society.

Proof of this lies in the scope and size of the semiconductor industry, where total revenues shot up globally by a surprising 26.2% in 2021 over the previous year, hitting a peak of $556 billion. The surge in demand was especially strong for analog devices (+33.1%), followed by memory devices (+30.9%) and logic devices (+30.8%). The year 2022 saw an additional rise of +10.4%, bringing the market's total value to $613.5 billion.[2] More than half of the industry's revenues and production are currently concentrated in Asia, with Taiwan, South Korea, and Japan taking the lion's share and China on the rise. In terms of market capitalization, the world's largest semiconductor company is Taiwan Semiconductor Manufacturing Company (TSMC), valued at over $500 billion at this writing. Actually, there are three contenders for the top spot in this industry in terms of turnover and revenues: vying with TSMC are Samsung from South Korea and America's Intel.

Generally speaking, the US is following on the heels of industry leaders in Asia while trying to step up semiconductor production after years of offshoring in that part of the globe. Driven by the fear that this strategic industry is being gradually pulled into China's orbit, the US has launched mega-investments in new production facilities, offering public subsidies to back the industry. Beyond Intel, there are other incumbents as well as newcomers on the American chip scene. The longest-serving veterans that are still in business include Texas Instruments, Nvidia (specialized in gaming processors), Advanced Micro Devices (AMD), and Qualcomm (with a special focus on the telecommunications sector).

---

[2] World Semiconductor Trade Statistics (WSTS), Semiconductor Market Forecast, March 18, 2022. https://www.wsts.org/76/103/WSTS-has-published-the-Q4-2021-market-figures-and-recalculated-the-Fall-2021-Forecast

For decades now, Europe has represented a prominent industrial pole for semiconductors, and it is growing. Thanks mainly to quality, creativity, and flexibility in its approach, Silicon Europe has taken on a vital role in the industry. The three main players are NXP, based in the Netherlands (which inherited Philips and absorbed the semiconductor production of other global brands, including Motorola), Germany's Infineon (heir to Siemens), and the French-Italian STMicroelectronics. Thanks to its worldwide scope, the European semiconductor industry, worth about $60 billion, can compete efficiently with Asia and America on all fronts, from design to production to distribution and sales.

Observing the world of chips from a European perspective offers keen insight and a unique vantage point. When we explore the histories and competencies of the "Lords of Silicon" in Italy, France, Germany, the UK, and other European industrial hubs for semiconductors, we find fertile terrain where we can forge a path that will lead us to an understanding of the inner workings of the microscopic brains that process the information of humanity.

The starting point on this path is clearly marked with a question: What are semiconductors and how are they made? To discover these secrets, we need to take a trip to a "fab" (the nickname for a semiconductor factory). And the perfect place to go to visit an avant-garde European fab is in the heart of the French Alps.

Inside the clean room

Crolles (in Val d'Isère, not far from Grenoble) is the home of the largest semiconductor hub in France, where 5,100 people work in a facility with a breathtaking Alpine backdrop. Here, the electronics tradition can be traced back to the 1950s, when a transistor factory was built by one of ST's forerunners (CSF) near Saint-Égrève. Today Crolles is ST's center of excellence for digital technology development and production, and some of these technologies, as we'll see during our journey, are among the most advanced in the world.

As in every semiconductor fab, all activity at Crolles revolves around the "clean room." But before we go inside, it's worthwhile to run through the entire process from the beginning. Better yet, let's start with the basics: What is a semiconductor?

Physics teaches us that semiconductors are materials that conduct electricity at an intermediate level at room temperature. In other words, they fall somewhere between highly conductive metals such as iron and copper, and insulators such as wood, glass, and plastics. Semiconductors have characteristics that make them essential in electronics; one of these is that their properties can be modified through a process called "doping" with other materials. Over the years, scientists have experimented with various semiconducting materials such as germanium, but since the 1950s they've focused on the most efficient one they could find: silicon.

Silicon is one of the most widely available and least expensive materials that exists in nature, because it's basically extracted from what can be found on any beach: sand. But to use it in electronics, it needs to be separated from the oxygen it naturally binds to by means of a complex physical and chemical process that outputs fine silicon crystals. For the chip industry, these crystals must be extremely pure. What emerges from the silicon processing plant is a silver-colored, circular section ingot, with a tip that houses the "seed." Once immersed in liquified silicon, this seed enables the formation of ultra-pure cylindrical structures.

But what arrives in the fab isn't the whole super-pure silicon ingot. Before getting to the clean room, the ingot has already gone through the delicate next step in the preparation process: it's sliced like a salami into thousands of super-thin "wafers" of mono-crystalline silicon. The classification for the fabs all around the world is normally based on the diameter of the wafers they process. As for the two fabs at Crolles, the more advanced facility works on 300-millimeter diameter wafers.

The byword for the entire process is *purity*: of the silicon (which can only have only one impurity per 10 billion atoms), of the air, and of the processing environment – hence the term "clean room." These spaces, which are classified by the number of impure particles permitted, are equipped with complex air filtering systems that work from the ceiling to the floor, producing a total air change in the room every six seconds. Every day, 24 hours a day, 365 days a year. Only

NASA's satellite production labs can compare to semiconductor clean rooms.

In ST's production centers, the delicate silicon wafers are processed in clean rooms that are thousands of square meters in size, completely sealed off inside the buildings that house them. Air temperature and humidity are kept at constant levels, and every clean room is built on pilings to absorb any vibration, including earthquakes. To access the clean room, personnel, who work eight-hour shifts, go through a number of steps, donning suits, gloves, head gear, and devices that make them look like astronauts on spacewalks. Even the water used in the production process goes through several rounds of filtration, making it the purest on Earth.

Ironically, one of the activities conducted in these super-pure environments is actually introducing impurities. Let's try to understand why.

A semiconductor can act as both a conductor of electricity and an insulator. The silicon atom has four electrons in its outermost shell, and none moves freely. This explains why pure silicon crystals don't conduct electricity at room temperature. To turn them into conductors, we need to add an impurity (a process called "doping," as we've said). Doping is done with a substance that has either one more or one less electron than silicon. Boron and phosphorous usually work best, enabling silicon to conduct negative or positive charges, depending on which electrons are released to move freely. With phosphorous (five electrons), silicon acquires excess electrons and becomes a carrier of negative charge, or a "type n" semiconductor. With boron (three electrons), gaps are created where the electrons were before, and the silicon acquires a positive charge, becoming a "type p" semiconductor.

It's precisely this positive/negative game that lies at the heart of all the work of transistors, which are built on silicon wafers to create the end result: a microchip. On a 300mm-diameter wafer, we can have hundreds or even thousands of microchips, depending on the size. Once these wafers are processed, they are sliced and assembled in plants around the world, in facilities that represent the back end of the production process. (The fab is the front end, and before that comes the design phase, which takes place in ad hoc research laboratories.)

A silicon construction site

Producing a chip from start to finish requires numerous processes that are done in clean rooms. Obviously, the type of processes depends on what kind of final product we want. First comes doping, then washing all the surfaces to allow the various strata of material to grow, followed by lithography, which lets us "print" circuits onto the silicon, and finally literally bombarding the chip with plasma to remove any excess material.

A chip constructed on a silicon wafer is a bit like a building. Let's imagine a building site, where the first stage is laying the foundations. Next, the ground floor, with beams and trusses. Then the first floor, along with the stairs and the elevator shafts, and so on. Building a chip is a similar process, but the order of magnitude of the components is measured in nanometers. The silicon wafer represents the foundations that form the platform holding conducting and insulating materials and metallic contacts – the various "floors" of substances that conduct or block the flow of energy.

The entire process makes use of lithography and chemicals to add or remove various layers, and to create channels, connections and pathways that serve to activate, deactivate, and "guide" electrons inside the transistor. But unlike a building site, it only takes a grain of dust or a microscopic particle of dandruff to ruin everything, which could mean wasting a single wafer or an entire batch.

Over the decades, ST has perfected its skills in this complex industrial sector, bringing together top researchers and creating labs and hubs for production and distribution all over the world. Today, ST is one of the world's biggest semiconductor producers, with over $16.1 billion in revenues,[3] and more than 200,000 customers. Of the over 50,000 ST employees, more than 9,000 work in research and development. It couldn't be otherwise, in a field where the latest innovation starts looking old in just a few months' time, and where competitors need to keep up with the frenetic pace of industries such as electronics, automotive, aerospace, bio-tech, and pharma.

---

[3] 2022 figure.

Mission control of ST's planetary network is in Geneva, in an elegant office building not too far from the international airport. The advantage of this location is that it makes life a little bit easier for the company's managers, who routinely travel to far flung places, everywhere from Japan to the US. At the helm of ST is President and Chief Executive Officer Jean-Marc Chery. The management team works under the Supervisory Board chaired by Nicolas Dufourcq, with Maurizio Tamagnini serving as Vice Chairman.

The Geneva headquarters runs a complex operating machine that counts 14 production and distribution sites and 80 sales and marketing offices spanning five continents. The front-end production hubs (where wafers are developed and manufactured) are located in Crolles, Tours and Rousset (France), Agrate Brianza and Catania (Italy), and in Singapore. The back-end (assembly and final testing) is split between facilities in Rennes (France), Kirkop (Malta), Bouskoura (Morocco), Muar (Malaysia), Shenzhen (China), and Calamba (the Philippines).

With some 18,000 patents to its name (and an additional 500 to 600 each year), ST products span a vast range of sectors. Its chips are strategic components for the digitization and electrification of automobiles, and also represent advanced solutions for telephony and telecommunications, renewable energy production, large industrial plants, consumer electronics, video games, and space research. If you take apart a mobile phone or disassemble a dashboard in a car, you will probably come across a microcontroller with an ST logo.

All you need to do is look at the top ten clients in ST's 2022 portfolio: Apple, Bosch, Continental, HP, Huawei, Mobileye, Samsung, SpaceX, Tesla, and Vitesco.[4] This gives a clear idea of the level of research and quality this kind of company needs, and the reason behind ST's strong presence in sales and R&D developed over many years in the US, Asia and Europe.

The picture we've painted depicts what today is a solid, global company focused on innovation. But it doesn't tell the whole story.

---

[4] As a listed company, ST is under obligation to publish its top ten clients; the list is in alphabetical order and not ranked by revenues.

Attaining the current organizational structure and level of performance was not a walk in the park. Far from it. The road that led to present day STMicroelectronics was paved with challenges, inspirations, difficulties, defeats, and rebirths. The story of this company is the story of a Silicon Europe that has never had it easy, the story of the evolution of microelectronics in France and Italy, an epic adventure whose protagonists are all too readily – and unfairly – forgotten.

To understand the twists and turns they had to face along the way, we'll retrace the steps in the technological transformation that changed the world, from the end of World War II to the present day. But we need to pick up the plot from the beginning, from a time of intrepid explorers who mapped out the path of electronics development on both sides of the Atlantic, setting the stage for the silicon revolution. To fully comprehend why in ST's fabs people walk around in space suits in clean rooms, and why smartphones have practically become portable alter egos for us all, we need to start from the very first brick laid in the foundation of the digital ecosystem: the transistor.

3   In the Beginning Was the Transistor

Bell Labs

In December 1947, Agrate Brianza was a farming town, for the most part, that still showed the scars from bombings during World War II. Meanwhile, on the outskirts of Paris, Puteaux was perhaps in even worse shape. Marshall Plan aid was about to pour into Italy and France, funding that had been announced a few months earlier by US President Harry Truman, as he touted the eponymous doctrine that was part of a geopolitical strategy to stop the spread of Communism in Europe.

While reconstruction was underway on the Old Continent, scientific research was business as usual in the US, which had been almost totally spared from bombardment. Enormous progress had been made before and during the war in electronics – not to mention physics. In 1945 the whole world witnessed the tragic evidence of advances in this field when the first atomic bombs were dropped on Hiroshima and Nagasaki. With these events, scientists became more aware than ever before of the importance of interdisciplinarity. Working together in teams was urgent and necessary during the war, but this method also proved to be an effective way to fast track innovation.

Bringing together a group of geniuses and putting them in one room sspecially adapted for them and for their ideas: this was precisely the purpose of Bell Labs. Initially based in New York City's Greenwich Village, Bell Labs later transferred their headquarters to Murray Hill in New Jersey, which became a state-of-the-art engineering hub, open to basic sciences and theoretical research too. The brightest minds, fresh out of America's universities, were recruited by Bell Labs and put in close contact with big brains from other sectors. This led to cross-pollination that would bear fruit in short order.

The most surprising discovery came on the afternoon of December 16, 1947: with a few sheets of gold foil, a piece of semiconducting material, and a bent staple, researchers built a small device that could amplify an electric current and open or close this energy flow.[1] This was the first transistor,[2] an invention born of the inspiration of a visionary yet controversial scientist, William Shockley. He had been hunting for new solutions to replace the precarious thermionic valves that electronic devices were based on at that time. Semiconductors became his obsession, as he was convinced that the solution he was looking for was hidden in their physical properties. But there was little chance that his theories would have taken concrete form if the managers at Bell Labs hadn't decided to partner him with two particular individuals: John Bardeen, a mild-mannered quantum physicist, and Walter Brattain, a high-spirited inventor-cowboy from the West who could solve any problem using the most unlikely objects.

This trio was an unusual one, but they blended in to their environment perfectly on the 80-hectare campus of the Bell Labs, modeled on the layout of a typical American university and filled with "mad scientists" who swapped ideas almost by osmosis when they crossed paths in the common areas.

Shockley was the member of the trio with the big ideas, the far-sighted theoretician who could intuit laws of physics that had yet to be proven. But he was difficult to work with because of his com-

---

[1] Walter Isaacson, *The Innovators: How a Group of Hackers, Geniuses and Geeks Created the Digital Revolution*, New York, Simon & Schuster Ltd, 2014.

[2] The bipolar transistor is an electronic device with three terminals (the base, the emitter, and the collector), controlled through current. By modulating the current injected into the base, it can be used as an amplifier, or in "on/off" switching applications to open/close electronic circuits. The name "bipolar" derives from the fact that the charge is carried on either excess electrons or gaps. The bipolar transistor works across a very broad emitter-collector tension spectrum, between 15 and 2,000 volts.

plicated, cantankerous character. Bardeen and Brattain took his input and worked on it themselves, nowhere near Shockley, spending all hours in the lab, running all kinds of tests. For days in that month of December 1947, they worked tirelessly on testing and retesting countless ways to control the flow of current in a semiconductor by inserting an electrode. They kept on changing procedures and materials again and again until finally, on the afternoon of Tuesday, December 16, success! A device made from a piece of germanium with two gold contact points installed on a spring. Brattain later described the discovery in these words: "I noticed that by careful manipulations I could obtain an amplifier able to increase the breadth of the signal hundred-fold, until it clearly entered the audio range."[3]

They had just made one of the biggest discoveries of the century, as their Bell Labs colleagues immediately realized when Shockley called them together a few days later. He had them put on headphones and speak into a microphone; their voices were amplified via an instrument made out of solid materials, not with a thermionic valve. But a genuine example of team effort this wasn't. In fact, Shockley, irate that he hadn't been in the lab when the successful experiment was recorded, immediately tried to come up with a scheme to claim the invention of the transistor as his own.

When news of the invention was released to the press, on June 30, 1948, it was described as the achievement of a team made up of Shockley, Bardeen, and Brattain (but the relationship between the three had already fallen apart). Not that the news generated much interest among journalists, who didn't initially understand what was so special about that little device. Indeed, the *New York Times* buried the story on page 46, among the day's trivial snippets of news.

The trio broke up quickly and came back together only in 1956 – when the three ex-colleagues were invited to Stockholm to accept the Nobel Prize for the invention of the transistor (an experience that Bardeen repeated in 1972, when he alone in the history of the prize

---

[3] Walter Brattain, interview by Alan Holden and W. James King, *Oral Histories*, American Institute of Physics, June 1964. https://www.aip.org/history-programs/niels-bohr-library/oral-histories/4532-1

won a second Nobel in physics).[4] At that point, the whole world realized the importance of that small device the trio had created. But it wasn't Bell Labs that could take credit for the popularity of the transistor. That feat was accomplished by a Texas oil company that decided to reinvent itself and break into the world of electronics: Texas Instruments.

A special radio

Bell Labs was modeled on an academic environment that fostered research and grand inventions, but it had nothing even vaguely resembling a business approach. For the transistor, for example, they discarded the idea of setting up production and instead licensed the patent to anyone who could come up with the $25,000 asking price.

If the heads of Bell Labs lacked market knowledge and savvy, as far as what might potentially interest consumers, there were others in America who had both in spades, and an entrepreneurial spirit to boot. Enter Patrick Haggerty, the man who ran Texas Instruments. His aim was to put as much distance as possible between his company and the grueling oil business. Not only did Haggerty buy the Bell license, he headhunted one of the Labs' best and brightest, Gordon Teal, a chemist who was studying semiconductors. Teal was convinced that transistors would be more efficient if germanium were replaced with another material he found fascinating: silicon.

As it turns out, Teal was right. In 1954, he announced the first silicon transistors, sparking enormous excitement among scientists and in the military industrial complex. But something more was needed to capture the attention of the general public: Haggerty's entrepreneurial flair. Not coincidentally, Walter Isaacson (the official biographer of Steve Jobs) compared Haggerty to the founder of Apple. Like Haggerty, Steve Jobs was no electronics genius either. His own version of Gordon Teal was his friend computer whizz Steve Wozniak,

---

[4] Bardeen shared his second Nobel prize with Leon Neil Cooper and John Robert Schrieffer for the fundamental theory of superconductivity, also known as the BCS Theory.

who came up with most of the first products that made Apple famous. But what people such as Haggerty and Jobs shared was the ability "to invent devices which consumers didn't yet know they needed, but that they would soon find indispensable."[5] What Jobs would later do with the iPod and the iPhone, Haggerty did in 1954 with the launch of the portable radio.

The invention was revolutionary for the times, because although radios had become the center of family life, nobody had ever dreamed of moving one, as big and bulky as it was, out of the living room where it always took pride of place. But Haggerty and Texas Instruments took everyone by surprise with the Regency. This portable transistor radio, which sold for the astronomical price of $49.95, was a huge success with unexpected consequences, especially in cultural terms. The little transistor radio, which marked the beginning of people's personal relationships with their electronic devices, allowed an entire generation of kids to listen to music in their bedrooms instead of having to share the family radio in the living room. Some have gone so far as to claim that the transistor radio gave rise to phenomena such as Elvis Presley and rock 'n' roll, which would have been unthinkable without it.

This is the reason why by the time Shockley, Bardeen. and Brattain went to accept the Nobel in 1956, the entire world knew what a transistor was. (Indeed, for many people, "radio" and "transistor" were one and the same thing.) Of the three inventors, it was Shockley who once again foresaw the long-term prospects for the device they had developed. Teal had demonstrated that the future of semiconductors was silicon and Haggerty's genius opened up new commercial avenues. Shockley converged these two ideas and saw where his future would lie: he left Bell Labs to create his own company that would produce silicon transistors.

The industrialist Arnold Beckmann, Shockley's biggest financial backer, had his business headquarters in Los Angeles, but the scientist refused to open his new company there. (The reason why still mystifies, decades later.) With his intractable, eccentric character on

---

[5] Isaacson, *The Innovators*.

full display yet again, Shockley stubbornly insisted the location be the town near San Francisco where he was born and where his elderly mother still lived. Until then its only claim to fame was its apricot groves. That town was Palo Alto. The opening of the Shockley Semiconductor Laboratory in Palo Alto in 1955 (the same year and the same area where Steve Jobs was born) is one of the milestones in the development of Silicon Valley as we know it today.

But this district would probably have taken off even if it weren't for Shockley. At the same time, in the very same valley, David Packard and his business partner Bill Hewlett were already hard at work. As were other companies that had been supplying the Pentagon since the war. And above all else, there was Stanford University, which continually turned out talented innovators. But what we can credit Shockley for was bringing to Palo Alto brilliant scientists to work at his company who would make history in the field of electronics.

One was an athletic 28-year-old Iowan named Robert "Bob" Noyce; many years later his biographer Tom Wolfe would compare him to the actor Gary Cooper. Another was a 27-year-old chemist with a calm demeaner and kind manners who went on to become one of the Valley's most highly respected managers. He even had a law of innovation named after him: Gordon Moore. Along with Noyce and Moore, many other talented people were recruited from campuses and companies all across country, and at Shockley this gradual concentration of ideas began to bear fruit. But the character of the company's leader soon proved to be a problem. For example, Shockley was obsessed with building a four-layer diode that might have become a precursor to the integrated circuit. Alone it could have done what several transistors placed on a single printed circuit would do. But with the silicon and techniques available at the time, the task was an impossible feat, and it immediately caused a clash with Noyce.

Shortly after founding his Lab, the news came of Shockley's Nobel Prize. This further fueled the inventor's megalomania. Red flags everywhere signaled that Shockley was veering dangerously off course in his private life. For example, he left his wife (who was battling cancer at the time) for a younger woman; he indulged his appetite for luxury sports cars. He risked his neck on daring mountain climbing expeditions, and his passion for magic bordered on the ridiculous. But above all else, he became interested in dangerous ideas about race, convictions that later made him a key figure in the field of eugenics and a spokesperson for American white supremacy. He even attempted to take these ideas into the political arena when, in 1982, he ran an unsuccessful campaign to represent California in the US Senate in Washington, DC.

It was inevitable that collaborating with such a character would soon prove problematic for the young engineers who had chosen to work for Shockley. Indeed, an underground uprising began fomenting inside the company led by a group of managers (including Moore), who began to scout around for investors so they could leave the Palo Alto firm. The turning point came when this rebellious group realized it needed a leader and they convinced Noyce to take charge of their revolt.

Traitors

In the history of electronics, they would later become known as the Traitorous Eight – the scientists who sank Shockley. But they were actually merely promoting what today we would call a startup. However, what was missing back then in the Valley were the venture capitalists who would later help launch dozens of IT companies. Encouraged by Arthur Rock, a financial analyst who believed in their project to create a company to lead the way in the semiconductor industry, Noyce, Moore, and the others eventually found the right investor. Sherman Fairchild, inventor and infamous playboy, controlled the Fairchild Camera and Instrument company and was the largest single shareholder at IBM.

With $1.5 million in financing and new headquarters defiantly located on the same street in Palo Alto as the Shockley Lab, in 1957 the Traitorous Eight launched Fairchild Semiconductor, among the preeminent electronics companies of the 20th century. This new venture would play a decisive role in the story of Silicon Europe, because not long after its founding, Fairchild would arrive in France and Italy (in Agrate Brianza, to be exact), partnering with Olivetti and Telettra to found Società Generale Semiconduttori or SGS (in translation: the

General Semiconductor Company), one of the forebears of STMicroelectronics.[6]

Fairchild's founding couldn't have been better timed: the Soviets
had just launched their first satellite, *Sputnik*, so in a state of panic,
the US suddenly realized that it had to fast track its technological development. Computers and transistors were the right recipe; semiconductors were the right path. But this time it was all about the space
industry, not transistor radios. Advanced technology and innovative
processes were needed, but most importantly, everything had to be
shrunk down to the smallest possible size – a real dilemma with the
number of connections that were required growing exponentially.

Back then, most of the work was done by hand-soldering components onto small, printed circuits. Aside from being costly and complex, malfunctions were very frequent when pieces weren't properly
soldered together. Two companies took the lead in developing solutions to overcome these limitations, and they achieved this goal in
different ways.

The first was Texas Instruments, and the solution was found by
Jack Kilby, another young talent who had passed through Bell Labs.
He was the first to figure out that he could build solder-free resistors,
condensers, and transistors on a single silicon fragment. He did this
by using impuritiesto "dope" the different parts of a silicon wafer so
they would respond differently to the flow of an electric current. In
1959, Texas Instruments presented what it called the "solid circuit" –
in actual fact, history's first integrated circuit. So began the era of the
microchip – though admittedly Kilby's solution consisted of a tangle
of gold threads that looked like a spider web, and it was difficult to
replicate.

A more elegant and efficient option was discovered around the
same time by the second company competing in the race to devel-
op the integrated circuit: Fairchild. It was mainly the inspiration of
Bob Noyce, but the trail leading to this solution was blazed by Jean
Hoerni, a physicist and engineer who had left Shockley with Noyce.
Hoerni began covering the surface of silicon transistors with oxidized

---

[6] See Chapter 4.

layers, protecting some areas while leaving others exposed. Working in this direction, Fairchild developed what would become the "planar process," laying the foundation for the method that is still used today for manufacturing silicon chips. Thanks to a property of silicon dioxide that blocked the diffusion of dopants, a layer of oxide could be grown on the surface of a wafer, but that layer could be removed wherever junctions were needed. [7]

With Moore's help, Noyce arrived at the same conclusion as Kilby about the possibility to create an integrated circuit with all the components obtained from a slice of silicon. However, Noyce developed a method that was much more efficient and replicable than the Texas Instruments approach. Here too, resistors, condensers, and transistors all coexisted with no need for soldering, but all the pathways and circuits were designed using oxidation and shielding processes, without all the wires on Kilby's microchip.

A legal battle soon broke out between the two companies, with each claiming the right to exploit the idea of the integrated circuit. Texas Instruments made the announcement first, but its patent was weak, while Fairchild's legal team described their process in detail and enumerated a wide range of uses for their invention. In 1961, the patent was awarded to Noyce, who was proclaimed the inventor of the microchip, but the legal battle raged on for years. In 1967, a verdict was handed down in favor of Kilby, which was later overturned in 1969 by an appeals court that ruled in favor of Fairchild.

In truth, Noyce and Kilby were always very generous in crediting the invention to the other, poles apart from Shockley's attention seeking behavior. In 2000, when Kilby won the Nobel Prize for the invention of the microchip, in every interview he gave due credit to Noyce, who had died ten years prior.

Another person who probably deserved a share of recognition was the Swiss physicist and engineer Jean Hoerni. "Hoerni's innovation allowed for a drastic reduction in the dimensions and costs of transistors, improving their performance," wrote Federico Faggin, an Italian scientist and entrepreneur who was one of the leading figures in the

---

[7] Isaacson, *The Innovators*.

silicon industry in Silicon Valley. "But above all else, he paved the way for the monolithic integrated circuit, which was the real revolution in microelectronics."[8]

The planar process opened the door to the possibility of producing more and more integrated circuits, each with an exponentially higher number of transistors, all on a single silicon wafer, with constantly declining costs. With this, the stage was set for the IT boom and the explosion of a phenomenon, one that a few years later Gordon Moore would describe in a study that became the basis for the famous "Moore's Law of Electronics."

In the meantime, silicon fever was spreading around the world and soon reached the other side of the Atlantic. Everything was ready for the birth of Silicon Europe.

---

[8] Federico Faggin, *Silicon: From the Invention of the Microprocessor to the New Science of Consciousness*, Cardiff, CA, Waterside Productions, 2021.

4   The Innovators from Milan and Ivrea

Floriani's brainwave

The transistor's potential was clear to researchers and academics from the start. But one of the first entrepreneurs in Europe to grasp what could be done with it was an Italian electrical engineer who was breaking into the telephony field, where he wanted to introduce an innovative approach based on electronics and radio systems. His name was Virgilio Floriani.

Floriani came from an area near Treviso, Italy (in the foothills of the Alps, in northeastern Italy), where his family farmed. Encouraged by his father, he was the first of his family to pursue his studies rather than work the land. Floriani graduated from the Turin Polytechnic in 1929 and gained extensive experience working with radio transmissions during the war. Leveraging this background, he founded a company in Milan in 1946. The name he chose – Telettra – reflected his desire to merge telephony, electronics, and radio.

In a backwards country, which Italy was at the time, the limited telephone network was based on old electromechanical technology that Floriani was certain he could integrate and develop thanks to innovations in the fields of radio and electronics.[1] From the outset, Telettra was a venture that focused on researching and developing

---

[1] Enzo Pontarollo, edited by, *La fabbrica degli imprenditori: Telettra e i suoi spin off* [The Entrepreneur Factory: Telettra and its spin-offs], Milan, Vita e Pensiero, 2002, p.65.

new processes, fueled by its founder's curiosity and openness to innovation. "My grandfather kept tabs on everything that was happening in America," says Virgilio's grandson, Federico Floriani. "And he was well-informed, for instance with *National Geographic*, which he subscribed to for many years. To this day we have more than 1,000 issues of that magazine at home, with its signature yellow spine. He got the magazines that Bell published too, and he read up on technological innovations."

When Bell Labs announced the invention of the first transistor, Floriani was quick to realize its potential. And when in 1954 Haggerty and Texas Instruments demonstrated what semiconductors could do in relation to the radio, Floriani saw that this was the future. In his 1980 autobiography, Floriani reflected once again, decades after the events, on the excitement he felt as he followed the developments in the US electronics industry. The invention of the transistor, he wrote,

"was a crucial step for the future of electronics. That little gadget, the size of a pinhead, there was no such thing as wear and tear if it was well-built. It replaced – with tremendous advantages – thermionic valves, which were big and bulky, expensive and unreliable, and don't last long. For applications in telephony, where the energy is measured in the order of milliwatts, the transistor is ideal. It took a few years before Bell's scientists managed to grasp and govern the laws and phenomena inherent to the new technology, and then roll out production. I was eager to get my hands on one of those little things."[2]

Those "little things" would become an obsession for Floriani, an opportunity to beat the competition, seeing as transistors didn't seem to be on anyone's radar in the European telephony industry. "I thought it was very important for Telettra, vital even," he adds in his autobiography, "to have access to, have control of a transistor factory. Since no one in Italy had thought of that yet, I decided that we, Telettra, would take the initiative."

So in 1955, Floriani did just that, and wrote to Bell to request a li-

---

[2] Virgilio Floriani, *Ricordi della mia vita* [Memories of my Life], Milan, Arti Grafiche Erreci, 1980, p. 113.

cense like the one Texas Instruments had obtained a short time before. He had already been collaborating with the labs, but the response he received went above and beyond all his expectations: in addition to being granted the license, he was invited to visit Bell Labs to see for himself the research they were doing. Floriani left for the US in 1956 and arrived at the famous facilities in Murray Hill to take part in the first symposium on transistor and semiconductor technology.

> "There were a hundred or so scientists and entrepreneurs from every industrialized country in the world," Floriani wrote. "My scanty knowledge of English and my ignorance of some of the theoretical principals of physics meant I didn't get much out of that symposium. But that didn't curb my enthusiasm: I realized that my job was solely to play the entrepreneur, and once I got back to Milan I set out to find a group of physicists who had the basic knowledge to tackle the problem."[3]

And so began a valiant, groundbreaking initiative, one of the first that would eventually build Silicon Europe. In 1956, Floriani set up a lab entirely dedicated to the production of semiconductors in a warehouse in Via Farneti, near Piazzale Loreto in Milan. Then, with the patents he had obtained from the US company Western Electric and from Bell Labs, he started producing diodes and transistors, initially using germanium and later silicon. The scope of the operation he set up was described in an internal Telettra report, "Technical Information Bulletin," dated April 7, 1957. Beyond all the photos of the building work underway in Via Farneti, the details about the ongoing experiment were announced to the entire company: "We have worked in silence for the past year and a half and now, on the occasion of the 35th Milan Fair, we will present our first products."

One of the surprises that was revealed in the news bulletin was the fact that Floriani opted to have his technicians on board throughout the entire process of semiconductor production. Not only physicists and chemists were involved, but also an entire metallurgical department, which was tasked with creating germanium ingots. As the Telettra publication underscored, "In the upcoming issues of our

---

[3] Floriani, *Ricordi*.

bulletin, we will update readers on developments pertaining to this marvelous new technique, which will be the cornerstone of all electronics of the future."

"How such a small company like Telettra could afford to run that laboratory remains a mystery to me. But [Floriani] built a team that wanted to do everything, starting with the raw materials," explains Guido Vannucchi, former general manager at Telettra (which he joined in 1960) and long-time close collaborator of Floriani. "In just one year, they even built the furnaces, and they worked on enhancing germanium crystals. But there was already a clear idea about silicon too."

The legacy of Camillo Olivetti

It didn't take long for Floriani to realize that the challenge was a daunting one, possibly too big for Telettra to take on alone. That's what was going through his mind right around the time when a company much larger than Floriani's got wind of what was happening in the labs in Via Farneti and wanted to find out more. That company was Olivetti, which was also on the hunt for semiconductors.

When it came to innovation, the Olivetti family, like Floriani, had been looking to America for decades. And it all started with an unplanned trip by Camillo Olivetti, the eponymous company's founder. In 1893, fresh out of the Turin Polytechnic, Camillo found himself in London where he was trying to perfect his English. One day he was called back to Turin by one of his professors, the renowned Galileo Ferraris (a researcher into electromagnetism and inventor of the electric motor powered by alternating current), who asked Camillo to accompany him on a trip to the US. Ferraris was slated to participate in the Chicago World's Fair and he needed an assistant and translator.

On their way to Chicago, Ferraris and Olivetti stopped in New Jersey to visit Thomas Edison's laboratory, and Camillo was struck by the great inventor. It was Olivetti's first taste of America, and his fascination grew as he continued on his journey to Chicago. After taking part in the World's Fair, the young man decided to stay in the US on his own. He travelled the rest of the country until he got to

San Francisco and then on to Stanford University, where he stayed for a few months, working as a teaching assistant. When he returned to Italy, full of the notions and innovations he had witnessed in America, he founded a company that in short order became the world leader in typewriters.

This connection with America continued when Camillo's son Adriano took the helm of the family firm. Under his leadership, Olivetti typewriters became a gold standard as far as international industrial design. The 1950 *Lettera 22* typewriter, designed by Marcello Nizzoli, actually went on display in New York's MoMA. Then in 1954, on Fifth Avenue in Manhattan, Adriano opened the first Olivetti Store, designed by the Milanese studio BBPR. The location was adorned with works by Costantino Nivola, the husband of Ruth Guggenheim and friend of Pollock, de Kooning, Steinberg, and Le Corbusier. The store had a place in the history of architecture, design, and marketing thanks to its innovative displays: typewriters were place on columns like works of art. But at the same time, they were accessible to everyone: in the space between the glass storefront and the sidewalk there was a *Lettera 22*, and any passerby could insert a blank sheet of paper and leave a typewritten love letter or greeting.[4]

"Olivetti was the first iconic Italian brand that really broke into the American market," says Luca Cottini, Associate Professor of Italian culture at Pennsylvania's Villanova University and creator of the website and popular YouTube series *Italian Innovators*. Cottini continues: "Many years later, the store on Fifth Avenue served as inspiration for the Apple Store, and the Olivetti style was a constant influence on Steve Jobs. It helped that in 1979 the Italian firm opened a research center right in Cupertino, not far from Apple. Since Camillo's visit to Stanford, there was a continuous connection between Olivetti and the USA."

At Olivetti they were thinking of America even when they went to look for Floriani, but they wanted help with a problem that had nothing to do with typewriters. For quite some time, and without drawing

---

[4] Paolo Bricco, *AO Adriano Olivetti un italiano del Novecento* [AO Adriano Olivetti, a 20th Century Italian], Segrate, Rizzoli, 2022, pp. 317–18.

too much attention, Adriano Olivetti was trying to take the leap into the electronics world, to keep pace with American innovations. Encouragement to do so came from none other than Enrico Fermi – the father of nuclear physics – during his 1949 visit to Olivetti's headquarters in Ivrea (near Turin). To sound out opportunities and scout talent, Adriano sent his brother Dino to open an electronics research lab in New Canaan, Connecticut in 1952. Dino began networking extensively, and made initial contact with Fairchild. When Adriano started looking for a scientist to entrust with the future of Olivetti's electronics development, the same name kept coming up from different sources. Both his Italian academic contacts and Dino in New York spoke to Adriano about a talented young man from Rome who was working in the US at the time. He had an unusual résumé, reflected in his Italian-Chinese name: Mario Tchou.

The Barbaricina School

Tchou was born in Rome in 1924, in the embassy of the newly formed Republic of China, son of ambassador Yin Tchou, who was so taken by Italy that he decided to give his firstborn son an Italian name. All of Mario Tchou's education took place in Rome, from elementary school to high school, and then engineering at La Sapienza University. He spoke Italian with a Roman accent but he had the distinctive Chinese traits of his parents. After travelling to China and Brazil, Tchou began working in the US and teaching at Columbia University. In 1954, Adriano Olivetti asked to meet Tchou at the newly opened Olivetti Store on Fifth Avenue, and all it took was a short interview for the two to realize they would be unbeatable partners in innovation.

Olivetti chose the University of Pisa as the ideal academic partner for conducting research in the field of electronics, and he tasked Tchou with assembling a team that would lead Olivetti into the world of electronic calculators. So Tchou picked ten very young researchers, and in early 1956 he took them to a villa in Barbaricina, a neighborhood in Pisa, to work. At just thirty-two, the Roman engineer was the leader and the most senior member of the group.

In 1957, after just over a year, a working prototype was ready: the *macchina zero* ("the zero machine"), officially named ELEA 9001. This was a remarkable result, one of the most advanced calculators ever produced at the time in Europe, but production required enormous valves and structures. So Tchou told the team that they would start over from scratch, but this time they would use transistors.[5] And thanks to the passion for outstanding design at Olivetti, the computer would also be redesigned with an eye to aesthetics – a task that Tchou assigned to a very young architect who was destined for a great future: Ettore Sottsass.

From the moment the decision was made to focus on transistors, the search began at Olivetti for possible partners. But this wouldn't exclude the possibility of setting up an in-house lab to work on semiconductors. Adriano once again turned to his brother Dino in the US for help, as well as his other brother Roberto, head of research in Italy, who eventually found out about the initiative of Virgilio Floriani.

"While I was reflecting on the problems that this new adventure would put on my already overburdened shoulders," Floriani wrote in his autobiography, "I had a visit from two young people interested in learning about our programs. They were Roberto Olivetti and Mario Tchou, both from the Olivetti company; they had only recently set up a division in Pisa dedicated to electronic calculators. To make a long story short, after I visited Ivrea – where I met the company's president, Adriano Olivetti, and the members of the board – we decided to join forces to establish a new company as equal partners: Olivetti-Telettra."   .

Vannucchi reflects:

"I don't know if Olivetti, with all the means it had at its disposal and the option to import transistors, had decided to produce transistors in Italy too. But perhaps the company found itself facing the problem of the exclusive license, which had been assigned to Floriani. It was probably a case of converging interests, which also prompted the decision to create a 50-50 joint-venture, despite the difference in size of the two

---

[5] Bricco, *AO Adriano Olivetti*, p. 322.

companies. I think [Olivetti] placed a high value on the lab that Telettra already had up and running and the Bell licenses."

Floriani was also given leave to pick the name of the new company and his proposal was immediately accepted. So, on October 16, 1957 the Società Generale Semiconduttori, S.p.A. (abbreviated as SGS) was officially established. The new company billed itself as "the first Italian company founded specifically to research, study and manufacture diodes and transistors."

Combining the research done by Mario Tchou's group in Barbaricina with the processes developed in Floriani's labs, the result was an avant-garde venture for Europe in technical and scientific terms, and this new enterprise had a new home. In the press release announcing the creation of SGS, Olivetti and Telettra revealed something more: "The large, ultra-modern facility of *Società Generale Semiconduttori* is nearly complete. It is located along Milano-to-Bergamo freeway in Agrate Brianza. It will be finished by the end of the summer and industrial-scale production will start immediately thereafter."

SGS's transistors accelerated the work of Tchou's group, and on April 12, 1959, the Olivetti company organized a presentation at the Milan Fair. The crowds were so huge that there was barely room to move, even though it was a Sunday. This was the debut of the Elea 9003, "the first Italian electronic calculator."[6] But behind this success lay the complications of running the complex industrial process required to produce semiconductors, the demand for which was on the rise. (The ELEA alone needed 300,000 transistors.)

"Semiconductor technology," recounted Floriani, "proved to be far more complicated than I had imagined, despite all my enthusiasm. Consequently, after a year, we considered the possibility of bringing an American partner on board who had the knowledge we were lacking."

Fairchild was ultimately chosen, and in 1959 the California company joined Olivetti and Telettra in SGS, with share capital divided

---

[6] Ciaj Rocchi and Matteo Demonte, *La macchina zero. Mario Tchou e il primo computer Olivetti* [The Zero Machine. Mario Tchou and the First Olivetti Computer], Milan, Solferino, 2021.

equally among the three partners. Olivetti and Fairchild, founded by the Traitorous Eight, had already been in contact for some time. In particular, a channel of communication had opened between Dino and Richard Hodgson, Fairchild's CEO and the numbers man whose job was to give some systematic order to the inspirations of Noyce, Moore, and the other brains in the group.

Fairchild had been established only two years earlier, following the brain drain from Shockley's firm. But the world of semiconductors was seeing breakneck growth, similar to what Silicon Valley would experience on several occasions in the decades to follow. It was time for Fairchild to expand too, and the company found an unexpected and surprising new silicon development center in Italy. Bob Noyce became a frequent visitor to Milan. ("I remember him when I was little, at my grandfather's house," say Federico Floriani. "He used to come visit us in summer.") And Richard Hogdson became good friends with Floriani and the Olivetti family – a friendship that continued with the next Olivetti generation and lasted until the American manager's death in 2000 in a car accident in Barbados.

A bridge opened linking Silicon Valley and Silicon Europe, and it seemed that SGS was in the right place at the right time, destined to join the ranks of the world's leaders in semiconductors. Another bridge, albeit a different kind, was also built at around the same time between France and the US, creating further conditions for the future development of Silicon Europe.

But things in the 1960s took a different turn. In France, because of public policy; in Italy, because of two sudden deaths.

5 The Pinball Scientists

The Latin Quarter Gang

In the history of the semiconductor industry in France, pinball machines played a key role.

One such machine in particular was especially popular in the 1950s with some young people in Paris who spent their free time every Saturday at a bistrot in the Latin Quarter. The pinball machine was the centerpiece of this little place in the fifth *arrondissement* that had turned into a regular hangout for a group of students and scientists. Saturday meant relaxing after a week of lessons and research in the physics labs at the nearby École Normale Supérieure, in Rue Lhomond. There were two things that attracted this group to this particular bistrot, and they would remember both of them for decades to come. The first was that source of mechanical amusement that challenged an entire generation of kids who had grown up during the war. The second was the chance to hear their teacher, Pierre Aigrain, speak extemporaneously, outside the classroom.

Few people impacted the development of the French electronics industry in the postwar period as much as Aigrain. If Floriani, Olivetti, and Tchou were the people who brought US transistor research to Italy, Aigrain played a similar role in France. He was one of that country's top physicists at the time, even though he had actually trained to be an engineer. As an added difference, and no less important, Aigrain was a pioneer in academia and politics, more so than as an entrepreneur. Because contrary to what happened in Italy, initially the French version of Silicon

Europe was above all a state-sponsored venture, with a strong accent on academic research and the military industrial complex. Most of the future leaders in the field in the 1950s had taken classes with Aigrain, and spent countless mornings with him in that bistrot in the Latin Quarter. The charismatic thirty-something professor was for France something akin to what Mario Tchou was in Barbaricina in Italy back then: a catalyzer of talents who were captivated by the new frontiers of physics and electronics. And like Tchou, Aigrain also owed his ascent to the US.

Aigrain's career path was meant to lead him to the French Navy. But he joined the Naval Academy in 1942, just a few days before the entire fleet was destroyed and had to be scrapped. Without ever having set foot on a ship, he fought in the resistance during the rest of the war, and after France was liberated, he was sent to the US, along with 200 other French Navy cadets. First, he studied in Norfolk, Virginia, then he went to Memphis, Tennessee, for training as a fighter pilot. But Aigrain was a clumsy genius, according to his students.[1] And a French officer on the base, Eduard Guigonis, noticed right away. (Years later, Guigonis would become a top manager in Thomson-CSF, one of the companies later merged into ST-Microelectronics.) So instead of becoming a Navy officer or a pilot, the then 22-year-old Aigrain was sent by Guigonis to Pittsburgh, to study at the prestigious Carnegie Institute of Technology (later Carnegie Mellon University). There, he earned a PhD in electronic engineering, but from the first he formed a close relationship with the department of physics and its director, Frederick Seitz, one of the pioneers of solid-state physics.

Seitz was impressed with Aigrain and brought him on to his team. In the meantime, the young French physicist Charles Dugas also joined them; he too was destined to play a vital role in semiconductor research. Seitz was struck by his tenacity: Dugas wanted to study Seitz's landmark physics textbooks – *The Modern Theory of Solids* – cover to cover, so he translated the whole thing into French.

---

[1] Philippe Nozières, *Tribute to Pierre Aigrain* (speech at the Académie des sciences, Paris, April 6, 2004).

Dugas had been circulating Sietz's ideas in France when the physicist heard what the young man was doing, and helped bring Dugas to Pittsburgh. But it was Yves Rocard, the director of the physics lab at the École Normale Supérieure, who really made it happen. At the end of the war, Rocard took over the Rue Lhomond offices after his three predecessors had all died in Nazi concentration camps: Henri Abraham and Eugène Bloch because they were Jewish; Georges Bruhat after being captured while fighting with the resistance. While he was setting up his new team, Rocard realized that what he needed was someone who would specialize in semiconductors, a field with great potential. He decided to entrust Dugas with this role, and sent him to Seitz.

The journey of Shockley and Brattain

This is how Aigrain and Dugas, the "two French kids from Pittsburgh," found themselves in one of the leading American research centers just as the semiconductor craze was reaching fever pitch. With Seitz's help, they assiduously followed the developments at Bell Labs and even crossed paths with the Shockley-Bardeen-Brattain trio. The mutual respect that grew from this connection prompted the Americans to turn to the two European researchers a short time later to solve a little mystery: Had the French invented their own version of the transistor? And if they had, did they do so first?

That rumor started spreading after Bell Labs made their announcement to the world in 1948. On May 18, 1949, the French minister for Post and Telecommunications (PTT) announced that a team at the Service des Recherches et du Contrôle Technique (SRCT) had built the first transistor in collaboration with the Franco-American company Compagnie des Freins et Signaux Westinghouse. The "transistron" (a slightly different name than the American version) was presented as the outcome of research conducted years prior (therefore before Shockley's team's work) by two German semiconductor scholars, Heinrich Welker and Herbert F. Mataré.[2]

---

[2] Antonio J. Botelho. "The Industrial Policy that Never Was: French Semiconductor Policy, 1945–1966," *History and Technology* 11, no. 2 (1994), pp. 165–80.

On both sides of the Atlantic there was heated debate on the transistor versus the transistron, but little was known about the latter. Meanwhile, Rocard called Aigrain and Dugas back to Paris to work in the Rue Lhomond labs. The two researchers had just discussed dissertations they had written, Aigrain on the Bell Labs transistor, Dugas on semiconductors and catalysts. So it was no surprise that the Americans turned to their two young French colleagues to learn more about the device announced by the PTT. Years later, the gruff, effusive Brattain told the story with his characteristic cowboy style:

> "Shockley and I got permission … to visit the people who presumably were the ones that were supposed to have done this. They were H. F. Matare and Welker … And when we arrived in France, either Aigrain or Dugas told us privately that these two men had no claim to have done this, scientifically, and they would be glad to see us, but they did not wish to discuss this question. So we spent the afternoon. After our luncheon with the PTT, with only wine and no water to drink. A big luncheon. I couldn't find a drinking fountain. I can remember this conference. Shockley of course was going great guns … I thought I was going to die if I didn't get some water! … We got some so-called devices … through some channel … and we measured them and they were just junk."[3]

Calling the first French transistrons junk was an exaggeration typical of Brattain, although the devices were clearly no comparison to the American invention as far as the scientific research that went into them and the technologies that were applied. But they did undeniably demonstrate just how much progress had been made by French research into semiconductors. The transistron was designed in a lab in Aulnay-sous-Bois, northeast of Paris in Île-de-France, where testing had begun in 1947. The radar industry was driving this research (in other words, the military industrial complex), as semiconductors were needed for sensors, prompting two companies to invest: Westing-

---

[3] Walter Brattain, interview by Charles Weiner, *Oral Histories*, American Institute of Physics, May 28, 1974. https://www.aip.org/history-programs/niels-bohr-library/oral-histories/4532-2

house (which produced semiconductors out of germanium, following the American process) and another firm with historic ties to the US, Compagnie Française Thomson-Houston (CFTH), which instead worked on silicon and certain other British models.

France's rapid access into semiconductors did not translate into a competitive advantage. In the 1950s, demand was primarily dominated by the military. The consequences of this were two: most of the research was secret and could not be commercialized, and it was mainly carried out in state-run labs. First among these was the Centre national d'études des télécommunications (CNET) – which also served to "filter" relations between scientists and the industrial world, at the time already impressive in size. In 1952, the French electronics industry employed 28,000 people, but the biggest customer (accounting for 37 percent of sales) was the armed forces, with revenues from consumer devices representing 32 percent of sales.[4]

In the years to follow, the semiconductor industry in Europe had all the right stuff to take on Silicon Valley, in theory at least. But it was thwarted by industrial policy that promoted the production of electronic calculators, but not their components, especially not semiconductors. This line of action turned France – and soon after Italy too – into a hunting ground for American companies, who could find very highly qualified personnel to manufacture products designed in the USA. In the late 1950s and early 1960s, IBM, Texas Instruments, and later Motorola all established their semiconductor production and integrated circuit assembly operations in France, just as Fairchild was doing in Italy with the joint venture with Telettra and Olivetti.

Major scientific research

What was lacking in industrial growth in semiconductors, France was compensating for in academic research, where the country was making great strides. In the 1950s, theory took the upper hand over practice in French electronics industry – in large part thanks to Ai-

---

[4] Botelho, *Industrial Policy*, p. 172.

grain and his young students, back in their regular hangout, that little Latin Quarter bistrot.

"I arrived in his lab in 1951 and the group became my family; we spent all our free time there," recalled French physicist Philippe Nozières during a memorial service for his teacher after Aigrain's death, in 2002.[5] "Aigrain would arrive every morning with a dozen new ideas. Many of them were off the wall, but there were always one or two that had serious potential. Coming up with one good idea a day is not something everyone can do! He would single us out and teach us this way, and it was tough going. It wasn't unusual to have to change the topic of your dissertation three times in a year. Aigrain was always giving us input, telling us about what he was reading. 'This solution should work, why don't you try it?' he would say. And we would enthusiastically charge ahead and face the unknown. Over the years, a wonderful bond was formed between teacher and students, one that rose above any hierarchies. He was a pioneer and our mentor."

In 1952, Aigrain found himself directing the lab on his own, because his friend Dugas had moved to the private sector to do semiconductor research: he had been recruited by physicist Maurice Ponte, a former student of Rocard who had become a manager. For years, Ponte was France's "radar man," and in 1950 he took the helm of Compagnie Générale de la Télégraphie Sans Fil (CSF). He served in this role until 1968, when the company merged with Thomson to become Thomson-CSF. Dugas was tasked with setting up the central research lab in Corbeville, which would take theory, based on the studies by Aigrain's team, and put it into practice.

In the French university system, a new type of course was initiated in 1955 to train future researchers: the Advanced Studies Diploma. (DEA is the French acronym.) Aigrain, together with Jacques Friedel and André Guinier, launched the DEA in solid state physics. From then on, nearly all the future leaders and top researchers in the French semiconductor industry passed through the classrooms of Rue Lhomond. And the École Normale maintained its status as the gold

---

[5] Nozières, *Tribute to Pierre Aigrain.*

standard for all the universities that sprung up after the University of Paris was divided into Paris 6, Paris 7, and Orsay.

An entire generation trained by Aigrain populated state-run labs and universities, as well as the private sector (Thomson-CSF, Radiotechnique, Bull, Alcatel, and so on). Thanks to his studies, the French physicist was recognized as a leading authority among Americans too, with whom he maintained close contact. In Nozieres' words: "I remember spending two summers, in 1955 and 1956, at Bell Labs; back then that was our Mecca. When Aigrain came to visit, I saw with my own eyes American physicists lining up in front of his office door to talk to him about their work and listen to what he had to say."

France too recognized the key role he played not only as a scientist but also as a manager in the public administration. Over the years, in fact, Aigrain held several government posts. He also worked in the private sector, and became the chief technology officer at the Thomson Group in 1974, where he did a long stint as a science consultant. In the 1950s, Rue Lhomond and Aigrain's labs were marked on the map of the nascent Silicon Europe, which, as we have seen, had strong academic, entrepreneurial, and personal bonds with the fledgling Silicon Valley and American research hubs such as Bell Labs in Murray Hill and Carnegie Institute of Technology in Pittsburgh.

At the time, this map showed little Italian flags in Milan, Ivrea, and Barbaricina, and in a few universities where scientists were investigating the physics of semiconductors. Instead, French flags were mainly clustered in and around Paris, at the labs of CSF in Puteaux, the research facilities of CFTH, the offices of companies such as La Radiotechnique and Westinghouse (among the first to attempt to manufacture transistors) and the Laboratoire Central des Télécommunications (LCT).

Another prominent flag flew in Saint-Égrève, near Grenoble, where CSF built a large semiconductor production factory that opened in the mid-1950s. The facility, christened by Maurice Ponte the Compagnie Générale de Semi-conducteurs (COSEM), would later merge with another semiconductor manufacturer, Société Européenne des Semi-Conducteurs (SESCO), based in Aix-en-Provence. The resulting enterprise was called Société européenne de semi-conducteurs

(Sescosem), another important piece of what would one day become STMicroelectronics.

On the map of Silicon Europe in the 1950s obviously many other flags were flying too, in countries such as Germany, the Netherlands, and the United Kingdom. Here companies such as Philips, Siemens and many others were conducting their own studies on semiconductors and embarking on transistor production. But France and Italy were already clearly on parallel tracks. This, along with their strong ties with the US, made a future French-Italian industrial merger a natural evolution.

This is why it's interesting that the final flag on the map should be planted in the foothills of the Alps, which divide (or unite?) France and Italy. In a place that symbolized the wealth of shared ideas and scientific discussions that connected Americans and Europeans as they broke new ground in the semiconductor industry. And where is this place? Les Houches, at the foot of Mont Blanc, near Chamonix.

It was here that in 1951 Cécile DeWitt-Morette launched her first global "summer school." A young French physicist who later emigrated to the US, DeWitt began a tradition, with the support of Yves Rocard, that still continues today. Her aim was to bring together the best minds in the world of physics, and the most brilliant students, in the Alps every summer; there they all could freely share ideas and do what today we call "networking." From the start, what would soon become known as the École de Physique Des Houches hosted some of the giants of physics, and saw a parade of Nobel laureates.

Taking the podium were the likes of Enrico Fermi, Wolfgang Pauli, and John Bardeen (one of the three inventors of the transistor). The students, in turn, would become future leaders in the sector, and many of them arrived fresh off Aigrain's courses, thanks in part to the encouragement of Rocard. The then 26-year-old Philippe Nozières was put in charge of running an entire summer session in 1958, hosting physicists from all over the world. The future Nobel laureate in chemistry Walter Kohn, who was 29 at the time, held a class on solid-state physics. As proof of the prestige of the summer school, and the strong ties between French semiconductor research and the military, in a few years' time the event was even promoted and financed by NATO.

In its early editions, the summer school lasted a couple of months, and participants gathered in unheated wooden shacks. Aside from lessons during the day, many climbing expeditions to Mont Blanc were organized: This was one of the activities that attracted teachers and students from so many countries. Mountain climbing has long been one of the favorite sports of physicists; Shockley is a good example (as he risked life and limb on several occasions). The history of European electronics and semiconductors was written in large part at these rendezvous in Les Houches. And it is singular and significant that it was a woman who was inspired to create and promote this event, especially in a scientific and entrepreneurial environment that at the time was almost exclusively dominated by men.

6 The Chaotic 1960s

Land of conquest

The 1960s were for Silicon Europe a time of great opportunities – and missed opportunities.

With the industrial activities and research initiatives that emerged in France and Italy, which were profoundly linked to what was going on in the US, there was the potential for a boom similar to what was happening in Palo Alto and the surrounding area. The ground breaking of the 1950s was led by the Americans, but the Italians and the French kept the pace with innovations, and they understood the vast potential of semiconductors. Thanks to the bonds with the US that had been forged by Olivetti, Floriani, and Tchou in Italy and by Aigrain, Dugas, Ponte, and Rocard in France, these players had direct access to cutting-edge industrial production and research. The stars of the transistor scene such as Shockley, Brattain, Noyce, and Moore, were frequent visitors to Paris, Milan, and the summer Alpine retreat of Les Houches. What's more, Europe's academic approach won the respect of Bell Labs, the Carnegie Institute of Technology, and Stanford.

And yet in the 1960s, from the role of co-starring with the Americans, Silicon Europe turned into a land of conquest and industrial colonization for them, a scenario that immediately set in motion a premature decline. There were many reasons for this downward spiral. In France, avant-garde centers such as CNET continued to concentrate on germanium for too long, before realizing they needed to pivot to silicon. In addition, production was dictated by dependence on the military industry, state support for academic research, and entrepreneurial activities that centered mainly on assembling electronic calculators. Substantial production of integrated circuits only got underway in earnest in the second half of the 1960s. But meanwhile, American companies (Texas Instruments, Fairchild, ITT, Motorola, Transitron) already had a solid foothold in France, and considered that country purely a place for producing and selling systems designed in the US. In 1966, for example, France was the largest market for Motorola in Europe, generating $2 million in revenues for that company's silicon components.[1]

The only industrial hub that could hold its own against the Americans was Maurice Ponte's CSF and its semiconductor district in the Grenoble area, which would survive over time and eventually be merged into STMicroelectronics. But this facility didn't yet have the capacity to handle mass production. What's more, at a time when communications were still complex, the 600-kilometer distance that separated it from CSF's labs in Puteaux was no small impediment.

In Italy, meanwhile, the Olivetti–Telettra–Fairchild alliance was showing promise. Floriani and his investors quickly realized germanium was not the right answer, and so they backed out of a production deal with General Electric on this front, and moved on instead to silicon with Noyce and his team. But SGS, which the Italians and Americans controlled together in 1959, was soon to be orphaned by two of its founding fathers.

On February 27, 1960, Adriano Olivetti – then 59 years old – suffered a cerebral hemorrhage while travelling on a train that had just crossed into Switzerland from Italy. Efforts to save his life were futile, and the world of Italian entrepreneurship lost one of its legendary leaders. At Ivrea, Adriano's heirs did not share his enthusiasm for the electronics industry or for innovative projects such as the one that Mario Tchou was working on with his team. Adriano's brother

---

[1] Pierre-Eric Mounier-Kuhn, "A History of Computing in France: A Brief Sketch," speech at the international symposium *Computers in Europe Past, Present and Future* (Kiev, October 5–9, 1998). http://www.icfcst.kiev.ua/Symposium/Pr_Content2.html

Roberto Olivetti was the only member of the group's new board of directors to believe wholeheartedly in investments in computers and in holdings in strategic companies such as SGS.

On November 9, 1961 (a little more than a year after Adriano's death), a decisive board meeting was scheduled at the company's Ivrea headquarters; this would be Tchou's chance to outline his vision for the future and explain why it was vital to stay focused on electronics. That morning, the engineer left Olivetti's electronics division offices in Borgolombardo, on the outskirts of Milan. Sitting on the back seat of his chauffeur-driven car, during the trip he went over his notes for what was going to be an extraordinary meeting: He intended to announce the results his work group had attained and discuss the possibility of building a portable computer. An avant-garde product which Italian industry could launch into the American market and win the same success as typewriters had before it.

Tchou was probably dreaming of the day – hopefully in the not-too-distant future – when he would see his computer in the window of the Olivetti Store on Fifth Avenue, the place where years earlier Adriano had interviewed him. But the board never had the chance to hear about his dream. On the Milan–Turin highway, the downpour was torrential that day. Near the Santhià exit, as the car turned onto the overpass toward Ivrea, the driver of the Buick Mercury Tchou was traveling in lost control. Swerving, the car slammed head on into a truck going in the opposite direction and crashed into a pile of rocks that served as a safety barrier along the side of the road. The impact was extremely violent, killing Tchou and his driver Francesco Finzi instantly.[2]

The engineer was 37 years old. His death – just one year after Adriano Olivetti's – sealed the fate of the Electronics Division, which was first disbanded and then in 1964 sold off to General Electric in the US. Olivetti also shut down its labs in New Canaan, breaking its bond with American electronics research. The tragedy hit SGS hard as well. "I admired Tchou," Floriani wrote in his autobiography, "as perhaps the most intelligent person I ever had the good fortune to

---

[2] Rocchi and Demonte, *La Macchina Zero.*

meet. There is no doubt in my mind that were it not for those two insurmountable losses, the future of semiconductors and electronic calculators in Italy would have been very different indeed."[3]

For some time, SGS seemed to be able to move on and grow together with Olivetti. The very young newcomers who joined the company at the time remember a stimulating work environment with a promising future. One such new hire was physicist Guido Zargani,[4] SGS employee number 35, who came on board in 1959 after Floriani had won him over. In fact, Floriani persuaded Zargani to leave Agip Nucleare, where he began his career under Enrico Mattei, accepting a contract that was for him a demotion, a step down from his position at Agip.

> "The person who arranged my meeting with Floriani was Professor Giancarlo Bolognesi, a prominent physicist I trusted immensely ... at that time, he was leaving the world of nuclear and moving to semiconductors at SGS," Zargani recalls. "Floriani told me about the projects they were working on and when I accepted the job offer, he told me: 'You'll see that these little three-legged crabs will revolutionize the planet.'"

The "little crabs" were transistors, the same "little things" that had entranced the founder of Telettra and convinced him to take the plunge into the field of semiconductors.

From nuclear energy to silicon

"Floriani was a great man," continues Zargani.

> "He immediately taught me something that has stayed with me all my life: how important it is not to sit at a desk all day, but instead to go around sniffing people out. He was quite a character! He would arrive at Agrate in an Alfa Romeo convertible, in shirt sleeves, and he would min-

---

[3] Floriani, *Ricordi*.

[4] Guido Zargani, who made a substantial contribution to *Silicon Europe* with his narrative, passed away in July 2022.

gle with our little band of chemists and physicists. There was nothing at Agrate, just a village with the SGS warehouse. The people from Olivetti had picked it as headquarters because the women in the area worked in the textiles industry and were extremely good at handling very small objects. In those days, assembling silicon transistors meant working with tweezers and microscopes, and they were perfect for the job."[5]

Bruno Murari, the future inventor of some of SGS's most successful products, came to the firm after leaving his post with SoMiREN (the Italian acronym for Nuclear Energy Radioactive Minerals Company), a division of Agip Nucleare in San Donato Milanese. Murari was also lured away from Mattei's nuclear adventures to shift focus to semiconductors.

"I began on November 15, 1961 – a few days after Tchou died," Murari recalls. "Everybody was talking about him and about the tragedy. One of my first assignments was to write up descriptions of Fairchild products. We would get samples from the Americans and we had to compile technical notes and applications notes in English; then 5,000 copies were printed up and distributed all over Europe. Fairchild wanted us to sell products that they designed over there, and we produced over here with the planar process. And very often we made corrections and suggested improvements to the Americans."

It was an intense time, and a chaotic one as well. The sector was exploding. Everyone was on the hunt for new clients and applications for the semiconductor industry, and everyone was racing to copy everybody else. Aldo Romano, who would go on to become one of the top executives at STMicroelectronics, joined SGS in 1965. He clearly remembers anecdotes from those early days:

"In the applications lab, we were tasked with testing the transistors and showing what they could do based on the applications notes. And at the time it felt a bit like the Wild West in that sense. For example, I had come up with some devices to convert direct current to alternating

---

[5] A company advertisement from that time read "From Lace to Transistors," according to people who played a part in the project.

current using Fairchild's first planar power transistors. There was one guy who came to check out these converters and he kept coming back again and again, always asking for more details. Later I found out he was taking my work and selling it – for a hefty price – to the Italian national railways, where they were using it to switch lights on."

But thoroughbreds such as Romano and Murari couldn't resist the temptation to analyze Fairchild's devices and projects, or the urge to modify them and propose new ones. At SGS, the desire rapidly intensified to leverage technicians' skills and build a path towards in-house research and development. But this wasn't what Fairchild was expecting from its Italian partner, which in the meantime had made a name for itself in the European market. During the 1960s, for instance, SGS had opened four more production hubs, in addition to the one in Agrate. In an interview at Agrate with the French TV program *Temps Présent*, the then-president and CEO of SGS, Renato Bonifacio, talked about the nascent Silicon Europe: "Clearly in electronics the United States still holds the lead over Europe. Here we need American technological experience, and SGS Fairchild was created with the very aim of exploiting US technological knowledge while at the same time preserving Europe's financial, commercial, technical and research resources. SGS is totally European thanks to its four subsidiaries in Germany, England, Sweden and France."[6]

It was Zargani who travelled all over Europe, opening one branch after another for Fairchild, planting flags on the semiconductor map.

"In 1963," Zargani recalls, "we realized that the factory in Milan couldn't meet our needs, so Bonifacio sent me to open a small factory on the outskirts of London. Before I got the chance to start running it as plant manager, I got word that I had to open another one in Germany, one in Rennes, France, and then move the one in London to Scotland. All of this while we were launching a testing center in Sweden. Between 1963 and 1966 we had a special kind of courage: to become European."

---

[6] Cyrille Beyer, *1967: aux origines de STMicroelectronics, fleuron européen des semi conducteurs* [1967: The Origins of STMicroelectronics, European Jewel of Semiconductors]. https://www.ina.fr/ina-eclaire-actu/1967-aux-origines-de-stmicroelectronics-fleuron-europeen-des-semi-conducteurs

In Rennes, SGS opened a manufacturing facility staffed by 500 people that would become an American stronghold in France. (Over the years, this plant would continue to be a production center for ST-Microelectronics.) With this plant, Fairchild had landed in France, like other American competitors, taking advantage of a weak local industry. The government financed CSF and encouraged collaboration with the researchers at CNET, but there was never a push to go beyond the production of conventional integrated circuits. Research on integrated semiconductors was also being done by General Electric, in collaboration with CFTH. This led to the first-ever commercialization of silicon circuits in 1964. An ad hoc company was set up to handle this new venture: SESCO.

But the French companies were only able to cover a limited market. So in the late 1960s, Thomson merged with CSF. Around the same time, SESCO also joined forces with COSEM (the analogous enterprise created by CSF), as we mentioned before. The new entity was named SESCOSEM.

The French landscape in the 1960s was filling up with initiatives and acronyms, but still fell short of the critical mass needed to compete with the factories opened in France by the Americans. Case in point: the creation of Thomson Semiconductors. To form this top French semiconductor company (which later joined SGS to become a true multinational), as many as 11 different companies were merged together from 1960 to the 1980s.

Meanwhile, America was surging ahead, spurred on in part by the Soviet Union's rapid advances in the arms race and the space race. In May 1961, US President John F. Kennedy challenged the country to send a man to the moon before the decade was out. Hence the inception of the Apollo program, which prompted NASA to acquire more than one million microchips, and led to Neil Armstrong finally setting foot on the lunar surface in 1969. The Pentagon also galvanized the semiconductor industry, investing in research on weapons systems and aviation programs (both requiring massive quantities of microchips), not to mention the new frontiers opening up in computer science. In 1969, a new program was initiated by the Defense Advanced Research Projects Agency (DARPA), the agency under the US Defense Department that was tasked with developing military technologies:

building a network of computers hosted by universities. ARPAnet, as it was called, was the precursor what today we know as the Internet.

Moore's Law, Faggin's trip

Unlike what was happening in Europe, in the US scientists were continuously inventing new applications for semiconductors, rather than simply producing them for existing industries. That meant instead of focusing solely on the space race or military projects, the Americans were exploring mass-market goods as well. And once again it was Haggerty at Texas Instruments who stunned the competition, building on the creativity of Jack Kilby, the inventor of the integrated circuit. A decade after the launch of the transistor radio, Haggerty replicated that success by inventing and marketing the first pocket calculator. Yet another case of a market pulled out of thin air but destined to last, even up to the present day.

At that point in time, American electronics appeared to be on a steady path. Every year the size of electronic devices would shrink, and at the same time production costs would drop and the computational speed and power would grow. In 1965, Gordon Moore of Fairchild published what was destined to become a landmark article in the magazine *Electronics*. In investigating these phenomena, he asserted that the number of transistors that could fit on a single microchip had more or less doubled every year up until then; he went on to predict that this trend would continue for at least another decade. A professor at Caltech dubbed this assertion Moore's Law, and since then it has become a touchstone not only of scientific research, but industrial electronics production as well.

Moore's prophecy was integrated over time to encompass microchip performance too: this, it was said, would double every 18 months, and prices would plummet. A megabyte of memory cost about €75,000 in the early 1970s, and Moore predicted that the downslide in prices would carry on over the coming decades. Today, the same amount of memory costs less than €0.01. So for half a century, the law intuited by an American manager has driven market choices, especially in semiconductors.

Around the time when he was working on his theses, Moore started feeling fenced in at Fairchild, like some of his other colleagues. The Palo Alto company founded by the Traitorous Eight from Shockley had lost its innovative momentum over the previous decade, turning into an outsized bureaucracy. Some among the original founders had already walked out in the early 1960s, opening what were later called "Fairchildren," companies large and small founded by engineers and managers who were former employees of the sector's leading firm. In 1968, Noyce began to feel a bit of wanderlust too, and it was clear that the die was cast for Fairchild.

Noyce convinced Moore that it was time to do something new. So once again, the two managers went looking for Arthur Rock, and asked him to assemble a network of investors. This time for Rock the task was a fairly simple one, because everyone wanted to put their money on the two people who had proven that they could build a global semiconductor colossus from the ground up. On July 18, 1968, Noyce and Moore signed the paperwork bringing the Integrated Electronics Corporation to life. But it's the abbreviation of the original name that would soon become famous: Intel.

A short time later, a third former Fairchild manager joined Noyce and Moore. His name was András Gróf, a Jew originally from Budapest who first escaped the Nazi purges, and later the communist regime. By the time he was 21 he had managed to reach the US, teach himself English, earn a degree *cum laude* from City College in New York, and then a PhD in chemistry at Berkeley. In the meantime, he Americanized his name to Andy Grove and started working at Fairchild. His move to Intel, where he became employee number three, marked the start of one of the most celebrated and consequential careers in the history of Silicon Valley.

It was not a very pleasant time, the years of upheaval at Fairchild, as some SGS technicians knew from first-hand experience.

"The atmosphere became heavy between us and the Americans," says Zargani. "In 1967, Bonifacio sent me to Palo Alto to act as a liaison between Fairchild and SGS – but I was actually sent as a spy. We wanted to expand, we wanted to do research and development too, and Fairchild didn't like it. So they sent me to try to dig up some of their secrets, since that was the way the semiconductor industry worked at the time. When Noyce and Moore left, the situation grew even more fraught. Fairchild brought in new management, seven or eight people who were so arrogant that at least half of my American colleagues walked out. There was a terrible atmosphere, and I found myself in the middle of a divorce between Fairchild and Intel, which would soon lead to Fairchild divorcing SGS too."

Faggin was also an eye witness to these events. This man – who would become the most prominent Italian in Silicon Valley – joined SGS in Agrate in 1967 after a brief stint in the US, an opportunity to study and learn how to make MOSFET transistors (commonly called MOS).[7] Faggin built the first two commercial MOS integrated circuits for SGS, and later the company sent him to the US to work at Fairchild. What was supposed to be a six-month stay in America turned out to be an entire lifetime spent in Silicon Valley.

"My first MOS product at SGS-Fairchild was a 16-bit static shift register," says Faggin. "At that time, MOS was in its infancy; we only made a few, but it began to develop its own small market. One of my strengths is my ability to make things quickly and at SGS I created the MOS process in no time at all. I must admit that it was useful to have access to Fairchild's internal publications on how to obtain pure oxides."

---

[7] The MOSFET (Metal Oxide Semiconductor Field Effect Transistor) has played a fundamental role in the history of electronics and therefore deserves a brief technical description. Whereas Shockley's original transistor was bipolar, the MOSFET is a semiconductor device with three terminals (gate, source, drain), but it can have a planar or a vertical structure. As it is voltage-controlled, the MOSFET is much easier to build, and use than a bipolar transistor. Conduction only occurs with unipolar charges, applying a given voltage between the gate and source. The MOSFET transistor is used in switching applications, or as a power amplifier in RF applications. It covers a very wide range of Drain-Source Breakdown Voltage values (the maximum voltage that the device is guaranteed to block between drain and source), typically from 10 to 2200 volts. The simplified control system and low power consumption made the MOSFET an ideal choice for replacing the bipolar transistor. This device also pioneered new, higher frequency applications which were not feasible through the bipolar power transistor technology.

Still a very young man, Faggin had started working at Olivetti, where he had been hired by Tchou in 1960 to design a small, transistor-powered calculator that would use SGS' first germanium semiconductors.

> "There was a sense of euphoria at that time at Olivetti," he recalls. "There were so many projects, some of them maybe even a bit overly ambitious. We all wanted to do so many things, and Tchou was one of those really hands-on people who gave orders and drove the process. Unfortunately, after his death Olivetti discontinued all the activities at Borgolombardo and sold them off."

After taking a few years off to get a degree in physics, Faggin joined SGS. The company was already very different from the one he had crossed paths with in the early 1960s. "There had been tremendous progress in semiconductors. Fairchild at that time had already made history by creating the planar process and abandoning germanium in favor of silicon. Then there were the first integrated circuits – a total revolution was underway. At SGS the working language was English, and they were setting up their own R&D department."

While breathing in this innovative climate, which was unusual for Italy, Faggin would toy with the idea of working at the American parent company. He was given that opportunity in February 1968. As part of an exchange program between Fairchild and SGS involving engineers and physicists, he moved with his wife, Elvia, to Mountain View. Faggin was immersed in a work environment where he was rubbing shoulders with the likes of Noyce and Moore (for a short time still), where Jean Hoerni had invented the planar process, and where the first monolithic integrated circuit had seen the light. The young physicist got straight to work, determined to make a mark by focusing on MOS transistors. And here he had the inspiration that would be his claim to fame.

Ten days or so after being assigned to the MOS project to solve a problem (to develop an auto-aligning MOS technology using a gate made of silicon instead of aluminum), he explained to his bosses Leslie Vadász and Tom Klein that he wanted to try an original approach, which became known as Silicon Gate Technology (SGT).

"The SGT that I developed at Fairchild is the technology that later truly changed the world," Faggin explains. "A new way of making integrated MOS circuits that twenty years later would allow all integrated circuits to be made with silicon gates. It's an innovation that lasted forty years and made it possible to reduce the size of all the components, to build all the pieces we needed to put a computer in a chip, to produce dynamic RAM memory and nonvolatile memory, which couldn't be done before – and finally – the microprocessor, which might have been feasible, but it would have taken three of four more years than it actually did."

The so-called buried gate invented by Faggin in those early days in Palo Alto opened up a new path to realizing the first microprocessors, which the Italian physicist would implement in the early 1970s. But not for SGS Fairchild – for Intel.

The break

The situation took an unexpected turn from 1968 to 1970. In June 1968, Faggin presented the silicon gate project to Gordon Moore, and at just 26 he found himself working on a team that was making history in electronics. His role was as an SGS employee on loan to Silicon Valley. But that same month, Fairchild announced it was discontinuing the partnership with the Italians. At that point Vadász offered Faggin a permanent position in the American company. He was scheduled to be officially hired on July 1, 1968. That very day, his first at Fairchild and no longer at SGS, Moore and Noyce dropped their bombshell: They were leaving Fairchild to found Intel.

Two years later, Faggin's patience had worn thin. At Fairchild, which had become bogged down with bureaucracy; it was taking far too long to develop his project. So, he joined Moore and Noyce, along with Vadász and Grove, who had also migrated to Intel in the meantime. And it was Intel that opened the door to fine-tuning the first microprocessor.

"I was tired of fighting to get Fairchild to adopt the silicon gate, so I went to Intel, which in the interim had copied the entire process," Faggin recollects. "They had all the formulas, they came up with their own process and I brought along two new inventions which had never been used at Fairchild. One was the 'bootstrap load,' an indispensable technology for two-phase logic circuits. The other was the 'buried gate,' in other words, the ability to create a gate buried in the chip and by doing so, to double the density of integrated circuits, with respect to what we could do before. It was a fundamental thing; it was what made the microprocessor possible."

So what happened between Fairchild and SGS?

Floriani, in his autobiography, has this to say: "The story of SGS in the years from 1960 and 1967 was marked by a rapid succession of brilliant successes initially, then mistakes, disappointments, inaccurate evaluations and mutual misunderstandings among all of us as shareholders." The founder of Telettra found himself in conflict with both Olivetti and Fairchild. The Americans, he explained, "wanted SGS to focus exclusively on production processes that were easier in technical terms, the ones that mainly used unskilled manual labor, and then they would purchase the semi-finished products. We Italians wanted to carry out the entire production process at SGS, to have control over all semiconductor technology. This was the only way the company could become autonomous." [8]

At the same time, Floriani didn't like the idea that Olivetti, after the deaths of Adriano and Mario Tchou, sought to leverage the collaboration with the Americans as a sort of "vanity project." Another thing that didn't sit well with him was the fact that Olivetti wanted to construct a large office building in Agrate, as they had done with the headquarters in Ivrea. Floriani later wrote in his autobiography,

"I disagreed with this. What frightened me was not so much the cost of construction, but the creation of the bureaucratic structures that inevitably would grow and multiply inside. Fairchild management was of the same mind. It was wrong of me – or rather, weak of me – not to take a firm stand alongside the Americans. The end result was that one day in 1968, I was taken aback by the announcement that Fairchild had decided to decamp, selling its stake to Olivetti." [9]

[8] Floriani, *Ricordi*.
[9] Floriani, *Ricordi*.

It's hard to say whether things would have turned out differently had
Floriani stood with the American partners. Fairchild bowed out because the company was pursuing new business strategies, and a partnership with an Italian company that was pushing for autonomy to
conduct its own research was not a good fit. Moreover, at Palo Alto,
the ongoing brain drain at Fairchild was spawning a number of "Fairchildren," while the biggest exodus of all was imminent – to Intel.
So Fairchild's priorities were poles apart from those of Floriani and
his team, even though the company was well aware of how much it
banked on revenues from European operations to balance the books.
In 1967, SGS-Fairchild and all its various subsidiaries tallied sales
revenues totaling 17.5 billion lire in Europe (25 percent in Italy and
75 percent in other countries).[10]

"There was always a bit of competition in this alliance from the
very start," says Guido Vannucchi, a former Telettra manager who
was very close to Floriani, "because the only thing Fairchild wanted
in Italy was production, while Olivetti and Telettra were pushing to
have SGS explore new terrain, run projects and ideate innovations.
What's more, the fight with Fairchild happened in a year when the
semiconductor sector had plunged into one of its cyclical crises, so it
was stressful."

Romano and Murari, for their part, remember all the passion that
they put into pitching new ideas as young project managers, and how
every time they hit a wall. The fact was that Fairchild did not value their approach. So in this respect, the R&D area that had been
created at SGS was facing a challenge. But an Italian market that
wasn't too keen on semiconductors left little room for maneuvering.
The lion's share of the work related to the TV and radio sectors, in
other words, traditional industries. Something similar was happening around the same time in France, where the biggest targets were
the military, along with radio and television. In both cases, Silicon

---

[10] Luigi Serrantoni, "SGS: dal transistor al microprocessore … una storia
che continua ancora oggi," [SGS: From the Transistor to the Microprocessor … the Story Continues Today], ComputerHistory.it, August 21, 2019.
https://www.computerhistory.it/index.php?option=com_content&view=arti-
cle&id=525:sgs-history&catid=16&Itemid=1050

Europe seemed incapable of inventing new markets or finding new applications for semiconductors – which is what Texas Instruments did in the US with the portable transistor radio and the electronic calculator.

At the end of the 1960s, on both the French and Italian side of the Alps, trouble was brewing. In France, consolidation was just beginning with the creation of Thomson-CSF and SESCOSEM. In Italy, instead, both Fairchild and Telettra had left the scene. After the Americans sold their shares to Olivetti, "I found myself in the minority," Floriani recalls, "and at odds with the majority shareholder. I didn't see any other option but to sell Telettra's participation in SGS to Olivetti. I signed the deal in 1969. That decision was the heartbreaking end of a dream for me."[11]

Vannucchi remembers Floriani describing that moment as a defeat. But it was somewhat softened by lessons learned on skills such as drawing up a budget, management control, and many other new business concepts that he had to deal with. But it was a heavy blow, that was undeniable. "Many years later, my grandfather described SGS as a great learning experience," says Floriani's grandson Federico. "But he would also speak of it with regret, the story of a failure."

While Silicon Valley was taking off, with Intel and many other big players ready to take the field, Silicon Europe was facing years of uncertainty and decline. Along with the bitterness that always comes with missed opportunities.

---

[11] Floriani, *Ricordi*.

7   Crisis and Rebirth

From fruit orchards to silicon

In 1971, *Electronic News* published a weekly column by journalist Don Hoefler entitled "Silicon Valley USA." In it, he reported on what was happening in the Santa Clara Valley, south of San Francisco, where the orchards in the area were disappearing faster and faster to make room for technology companies. From Palo Alto to San José, via Mountain View, Sunnyvale, Cupertino, and Santa Clara, new silicon companies were sprouting up everywhere, often founded by young people fresh out of Stanford, the local university. Either that or they started out at Hewlett-Packard, Shockley, Fairchild, or one of the many "Fairchildren." As Bell Labs had done before on the east coast, Xerox Corporation opened a lab in 1970 called Xerox PARC. With an exclusive focus on research, this facility became a pole of attraction for tech experts from all over the country.

This was the launch of Silicon Valley as we know it today. And the name Hoefler had given it was destined to become a global brand. This frenzied explosion of the Valley was fueled by a one-of-a-kind, once-in-a-lifetime amalgam of high-level engineering mixed with entrepreneurial culture cultivated at Stanford, and a sprinkling of youthful rebellion against authority that was critical of the traditional rigid corporate structures. Added to this combustible combination was a bit of everything: the hippy culture, experiments with drugs, anti-establishment attitudes, pacifism (to counter the Vietnam War), creativity sparked by contamination between technology, and a humanistic culture. And the bible for all this was the cult magazine *Whole Earth Catalog*.

Silicon Valley became the place where everything seemed possible and anything could be done. Technological advances often started as forms of entertainment, games that evolved in the emerging hacker culture, to eventually turn into innovation accelerators. If in France the semiconductor school was founded on the passion for pinball, in America the path to the future domination of software over hardware was paved by a videogame invented in academic circles in the 1960s. That game – Spacewar – became an obsession for thousands of computer geeks, and in 1972 in Sunnyvale, California, it led to the birth of a company that would revolutionize the habits of an entire generation: Atari.

With the moon landing in 1969, space suddenly wasn't so "far out." It provided inspiration for everyone and prompted young Californians such as George Lucas to invent incredible worlds and experiment with new digital technologies to tell their stories. When *Star Wars* debuted in theaters in 1977, the Silicon Valley generation found its very own space epic.

For gaming – and for thousands of other things – the first personal computers were about to arrive, just what Mario Tchou had been aspiring to but never had the time to make. The predecessor of all PCs was called Altair, a name borrowed from *Star Trek*, another space saga. In 1974, when it was featured on the cover of *Popular Electronics*, Altair instantly became the object of desire of two kids who weren't too good at hardware, but who dreamed about building and programming software: their names were Bill Gates and Paul Allen.

They cut their teeth writing software programs for two years with a gizmo they bought in a shop for $360: a semiconductor that had ignited the entire revolution that was engulfing the Valley.[1] It was the Intel 8008, one of the first microprocessors in the world and the forefather of the successful X86 family. This jewel had been crafted by Faggin, among others, so in a certain sense it also carried the ge-

---

[1] Paul Allen, *Idea Man: A Memoir by the Cofounder of Microsoft*, Alberta, Portfolio, 2011.

netic code of SGS-Fairchild. The managers of the electronics shop, in Gates's words, "couldn't believe it. Two kids coming in and buying an 8008. And we were so worried as we unwrapped the foil that we would break the thing."[2]

The name "microprocessor" reflected the fact that it was a computing processor installed on a chip. The world's first, the 4004, was presented by Intel in November 1971 with a two-page advertisement in *Electronic News*. The eye-catching headline: "Announcing a new era in integrated electronics." And this was no exaggeration – it really was a revolution. A programmable chip that could perform any logic-based function was a giant leap forward from single-function chips. The microprocessor opened the gate for the imminent software boom. Suddenly the technicians started playing a central role because they knew how to program the instructions to tell the system what to do.

Faggin realized that something special was happening in the Valley; there he would have opportunities he wouldn't get in Europe. This was one reason why he stayed in the US and found himself taking a front row seat in the history of electronics. "In Italy, things moved slowly," he says, "while in America they moved fast. And when they didn't move fast enough, you could go to another, faster company. That's what I did when I left Fairchild for Intel."

The microprocessor was inspired by an intuition that was also in some sense a wager. The Japanese company Busicom had asked Intel to design twelve specific microchips, each to perform a specific function, in a desktop calculator it was building. To tackle this project, Bob Noyce tasked the team led by Ted Hoff, a young teacher from Stanford and a new hire at Intel. It was Hoff, along with Noyce, who came up with the idea of building a multipurpose chip that could be programmed like a computer. This chip could handle most of the functions that Busicom wanted from the twelve different devices. The wager was whether or not this was feasible, and it was up to Faggin, who had just joined the team, to turn this possibility into a reality.

---

[2] Walter Isaacson, *The Innovators*.

They won the bet, and Intel 4004 paved the way for creating more sophisticated microprocessors, such as the 18-pin 8008 and then the 8080, which would ring in the second generation of microprocessors announced in 1974. Motorola quickly followed suit, debuting its own 8-bit 6800 model.

The paranoid company

In no time at all, Intel was leading the way into a new world, and it had done so thanks in part to its own unique corporate culture, which was very different from Shockley's and Fairchild's, where it had originated. Noyce built Intel on solidly egalitarian foundations, and Moore nurtured its long-term vision. But it was Andy Grove who shaped and guided the company, using an approach that is perfectly encapsulated in the title of his future bestseller, *Only the Paranoid Survive*. Writer Tom Wolfe, when telling the Intel story in his profile of Noyce, offered an enduring insight: "This wasn't a corporation ... it was a congregation."[3]

> "Andy Grove was the company's most powerful driving force," Faggin confirms. "He was the one who created the Intel culture, much more so than Noyce and Moore. It was something completely novel. Intel had in some sense fused together an entrepreneurial culture and the ability to make products that were totally new. If you look at the early Intel products, what strikes you is that they are all things that had never been made before."

Thanks to Faggin's microprocessor and the acceleration it set in motion, it was all systems go for the launch of the era of personal computers and software. Soon Bill Gates and Paul Allen would open Microsoft, and the IBM standard for office machines would spread like lightning around the world. But it was a boom that Europe could only watch from the sidelines, with no chance of getting on the field

---

[3] Tom Wolfe, "The Tinkerings of Robert Noyce. How the Sun Rose on Silicon Valley," *Esquire* (December 1983), pp. 346–74.

to play. Meanwhile, aggressively forcing its way onto the electronics scene was Japan.

As far as transistors and the beginnings of the semiconductor industry, Silicon Europe kept up with the US fairly well in the 1950s and 1960s. But the situation changed in the decade when the Valley in America started to flourish. In Italy, Olivetti could have ridden the wave, but after the death of Adriano Olivetti and Tchou, the Ivrea-based company went back to typewriters (which would soon be converted to electric) and calculators that used mechanical technology, for the most part. Management wasn't convinced about electronics or digital technology, so they discontinued the computer project.[4]

> "At that time," comments Faggin, "Olivetti didn't see how important software was. In other words, for them the computer was just hardware, and for software, 'you do it later, when you need it.' But that's not how it worked. IBM had already been in the business for ten years and understood the problem, and was tackling it by bringing a family of computers to market called System/360. It had the first operating system, the first computer that truly made history. It changed the very architecture for making computers. And all this was accelerated by the microprocessor."

After retreating from the front lines of electronics, Olivetti also gradually lost interest in semiconductor production. After Fairchild left the scene, and later Floriani with his Telettra, the Ivrea-based group looked for new partners to bring on board SGS. It was the late 1960s, and two candidates emerged: Fiat, and even more promising, IRI, the giant Italian public holding company that was bringing together a large part of Italian industrial policy.

---

[4] Shortly before the sale of Olivetti, Tchou's former division had actually produced a personal computer, the Programma 101, designed by Pier Giorgio Perotto. Several versions were developed (including the P6040 in 1975, based on Intel's 8080 microprocessor), but conviction was lacking in the company, as was the marketing campaign needed to turn it into a flagship product.

All alone in Agrate

In Agrate, this was a vulnerable time for SGS. With Americans gone, the Italians had far more maneuvering room, and they exploited it to set up their own research and development lab specifically to work on planar silicon integrated circuits. The company had grown to an impressive size, with 2,500 employees and six production units.[5] SGS (which at that time meant Olivetti too) had factories in the rest of Europe as well, facilities that Fairchild had offloaded. So Silicon Europe emerged thanks to the links between Agrate and the various production centers scattered across the continent and the network that had formed among them.

European expansion coincided with the company's arrival in Asia in 1969. Studying how the Americans at Fairchild were doing business, the Italians noticed that the Silicon Valley company was reaping the rewards of its decision to open a branch in Hong Kong. What's more, Asia represented both a huge market and a production site with much lower costs than in Europe.

"We imitated Fairchild a little bit," Zargani says. "An SGS manager toured around Asia and ended up choosing Singapore as the ideal location. Olivetti had already a business up and running there, and this was seen as an advantage, because it gave us a foothold, a place to start. So, on March 30, 1969, they put me on a plane and I went to start up our project in Singapore. At the time, it was such a long trip! You departed from Rome with Alitalia and then had a layover in Bombay. From there you took another flight to Ceylon or Bangkok, then a third flight to Singapore, where there was an old airport, nothing like the current one. Singapore turned out to be a very smart choice. Many people followed our lead, but SGS arrived first and laid the foundations for a solid, lasting relationship with the local authorities. When I arrived, I didn't know anyone except the head of the local Olivetti office, Enrico Miserendino;

---

[5] Sylvie Daviet, *"Emergence et structuration d'une multinationale européenne du semi-conducteur: le cas de ST Microelectronics"* [Emergence and Structure of a European Semiconductor Multinational: The Case of ST Microelectronics], *Annales de Géographie* 109, no. 612 (2000), pp. 132–51.

we remained friends all our lives. By the 29th of the following April, we had already opened the SGS offices."

The approach that SGS chose, Zargani continues, was the same one that the Italian company had adopted with Fairchild to expand in Europe: opening "temporary factories" wherever there was available space, growing them, and then moving them to permanent locations.

"In Rennes, France, we chose a school, in Scotland it was a movie theater. In Singapore we were lucky because they had set up buildings specifically to accommodate Western companies. I brought in six young technicians and together we built everything. To give you an idea of the scale of the undertaking, when Fairchild and Texas Instruments arrived in Singapore some time later, they both disembarked from ships with around 80 people and all the equipment on board."

For SGS and for the future STMicroelectronics, opening the Singapore branch marked a milestone in the company's history, the start of an Asian adventure that still continues to this day. But at the time, when SGS wasn't sailing in smooth waters, it meant upping production efforts and costs. Then in 1970, crisis struck the semiconductor industry (as it did periodically) and SGS wound up in the red. Prospects couldn't be worse, because the majority shareholder was distracted and the arrival of microprocessors had caught Agrate by surprise. So SGS had no other choice than to produce them under license, on behalf of the Americans.

When its new partner IRI came on the scene, SGS was pulled it into the orbit of STET, the conglomerate in which the state-owned colossus had united all its telecommunications and IT companies. Under this umbrella there was already a semiconductor manufacturing company called ATES, which had been in business as long as SGS more or less, and had followed a path similar to Floriani & Co.

ATES was founded in L'Aquila in 1959 under the name ELIT-Elettronica Italiana for the production of thermionic valves. The company later expanded into semiconductors and changed its name to reflect this: ATES-Aquila Tubi Elettronici e Semiconduttori. In 1961, not long after Fairchild came on board in SGS, ATES also sought out and eventually found an American partner, RCA, which initially granted the Italian company a license to manufacture thermionic valves. The pivot in production to the semiconductor sector prompted ATES and RCA to open a new plant. For the location, Catania was chosen, where ATES-Componenti Elettronici SpA was set up in 1963. RCA provided the technology, and the work mainly consisted of assembling semi-finished products shipped over from the American plant in Findlay, Ohio.[6] The diodes and transistors produced in Catania were initially made of germanium, and then mainly silicon; the plant produced capacitors and resistors as well.

So SGS and ATES shared similar backgrounds and faced the same basic problem: throughout the 1960s, an entire decade spent making products for the Americans, they couldn't get proprietary research activities up and running. At some point the Americans stepped back from ATES too, and as at SGS, this was seen as an opportunity to finally start R&D in earnest. To do so, ATES opened a research center in the Castelletto district of Cornaredo, a town not far from Milan and Agrate.

The company had a hybrid public and private ownership structure, with STET holding controlling interest and participation by Germans from Siemens. The company expanded from 352 employees in 1967 to 2,058 in 1970, when the global crisis in the semiconductor industry struck ATES as well. IRI's response was to merge two fragile, vulnerable enterprises into a single Italian semiconductor company, SGS-ATES Componenti Elettronici SpA. The merger was finalized on December 29, 1972, and the new entity was controlled by IRI-STET, as a 60 percent majority shareholder; Olivetti and Fiat each held 20 percent of the share capital.

The sun had set once and for all on the vision of Adriano Olivetti, Virgilio Floriani, and Mario Tchou, and so began a tumultuous decade for SGS-ATES. The situation at IRI was equally critical. In 1976, it set an unenviable record: all its public sector companies closed in the red.

---

[6] Serrantoni, *SGS*.

Grenoble takes off

The French front of Silicon Europe was facing similar challenges. Thomson-CSF had merged all its semiconductor production activities in the newly created SESCOSEM, while the two production centers in Saint-Égrève (near Grenoble) and Aix-en-Provence remained operational. But here too, most of the production was for American clients, in particular IBM. To keep production running and avoid having to close one of the two plants, it took continuous injections of public funds.

In France, as in Italy with IRI, public subsidies were shoring up a sizeable portion of the electronics sector, with priority resting with production relating to consumer goods (primarily television and radio). At the same time, the French approach consistently embraced a strong commitment to academic research. Since Aigrain and Dugas set up their first labs, this support made it possible to keep pace with American innovations on a scientific level. But a strong private sector market was lacking, in contrast to what was happening in Silicon Valley. This explains why the high-profile public research center LETI, the French answer to Xerox's PARC, had been struggling for some time to collaborate effectively with private enterprise. LETI (short for Laboratoire d'Électronique et de Technologie de l'Informatique) was opened in 1967 as a division of CEA (Commissariat à l'énergie atomique et aux énergies alternatives). Headquarters for the research hub were established at the University of Grenoble, making the Alpine city the epicenter for microelectronics, integrated circuits, and the study of semiconductors in France.

Initially, there was little collaboration between Thomson (and its affiliate SESCOSEM) and LETI because the focus of the latter was purely scientific. But that changed when Grenoble Laboratories decided to initiate a project specifically aimed at industrial partnerships. It was called Étude et Fabrication de Circuits Intégrés Spéciaux (The Study and Production of Special Integrated Circuits), but since the French love their acronyms, it soon became known simply as EFCIS. The focus of the project from the outset was to specialize in MOS integrated circuits. This prompted Thomson to become a shareholder in 1976, and later to obtain a controlling interest. What started in

Grenoble with the work of EFCIS set a process in motion that years later would represent a crucial comeback, a chance to catch up with the Americans as far as embedded processing solutions with microprocessors and image sensors: two fields in which France took the lead.

The microcontroller is in a certain sense an evolution of the microprocessor invented by Intel. If we take a single chip and, along with the processor, we add support circuits, memory, and input/output peripherals, we get a microcontroller. It's really an electronic brain capable of handling myriad operations and processes. Since the 1970s, microcontrollers have been invading the sphere of consumer electronics, from TVs to household appliances. What's more, these devices have become critical components in various industries: automotive, telephony, and finally in the sphere of smart cards. The chips on our credit cards, in our phone's SIM card, or in our hotel room passkey, function thanks to microcontrollers, for the most part.

France – and, specifically, the company that would eventually become STMicroelectronics – ultimately succeeded in surpassing Intel to take the lead in MCUs. And this success is in part thanks to the competencies that were built on another first-time achievement, one dating back to the 1970s. For years it was just a French thing, but eventually it conquered the world. We're talking about the invention of smart cards, which today are concentrations of microcontroller technology. It was a success attributed to an unusual character who deserves worldwide fame: Roland Moreno.

Moreno, who died in 2022 at the age of 66, was born in Cairo, Egypt. His last name was originally Bahbout, but the family changed it when they moved to France, when the future inventor was a young child. For many years, Moreno didn't know what to do with his life. He worked for a time as a journalist, and tried on many other hats as well. He had a gift of a subtle irony, so he even toyed with the idea of a career as a comedian. His hero was Woody Allen; they shared similar cultural roots, both being Jewish, and even a similar look, right down to their hair.

The turning point for Moreno came when he decided to set up a company, Innovatron. After selling various kinds of ideas and patents, Innovatron got the break of a lifetime with a strike-it-rich project: a chip that would allow people to carry their personal data with them at all times. (Moreno claimed he saw this chip in a dream.) The first versions of what would later become the "smart card" was patented by Moreno in 1974. A few years later came the most promising prototype, placing the chip of the smart card on a plastic card. The code name for the product was TMR, taken from the title of the Woody Allen movie, *Take the Money and Run*.

The *"carte à puce,"* as it became known in France, was a huge hit there, but for many years it never spilled over that country's borders. The national phone company, France Télécom, began selling phone cards embedded with Moreno's chip, and French banks followed suit. Soon France found itself blazing the trail for what would become a global phenomenon, albeit one that had a slow start. American Express was among the first big multinationals to insert the chip in its credit cards, turning them into smart cards, but not until 1999. Soon the entire world followed AmEx's lead, and chip-embedded smart cards laid claim to bank cards, SIM cards in cellphones, passports and ID cards, company badges and supermarket loyalty club cards: Moreno's chip was everywhere, and still is today.

And all these smart cards worked thanks to microcontrollers.

The world leader in this field for many years was Motorola, and when EFCIS began to collaborate with the American company, Grenoble also broke into the segment of microcontrollers. Claude Dardanne, a manager who began his career at EFCIS in the 1970s, stayed with Thomson after the buyout, where he began working on MCUs. We have already met Dardanne at the beginning of our journey into the world of semiconductors. After a six-year hiatus at Apple, he returned to STMicroelectronics to lead the charge in the company's comeback, lifting it up from twelfth to first place in the world in the field of general-purpose microcontrollers. It had been a long road that started out in the early years of LETI and EFCIS.

Microcontrollers and image sensors, which we will find again along the way in our journey through Silicon Europe, were positive exceptions in a French electronics industry that suffered from growing dependence on US-produced components. An illuminating example is Compagnie Internationale pour l'Informatique (CII, later Honeywell-Bull, and later still simply Bull), a company created by the De Gaulle government in 1966 as part of a national action plan to foster French info-tech development. When in 1971 CII presented its new generation computers, it turned out that 90 percent of the integrated circuits, the nuts and bolts of these machines, were made in the US, for the most part by Texas Instruments.

To give impetus to the French industry, during the 1970s the government launched a new series of public incentives, the Plan Composants (Components Plan), in an attempt, at minimum, to shore up the relationship with the Americans and put the two countries on par. It was within the framework of this program that EFCIS teamed up with Motorola, a partnership which later moved into the orbit of Thomson. At the same time, in Rousset (Provence), on the initiative of Saint-Gobain and National Semiconductor, Eurotechnique was established. This new company would soon become another building block that would form the foundations of STMicroelectronics.

The silicon cowboys have their day

During the 1970s crisis, the poor performance of the semiconductor industry in Italy and France did have one silver lining: It forced the players to be creative. The Americans were dominating the boom in computers and computer software, this had quickly become clear. They were now untouchable in that competitive arena. But in electronics and industrial production in general, semiconductors played a critical role in many other areas as well.

The Grenoble hub began to specialize in products for digital telephony and image management, focusing primarily on production for the television sector. But in doing so, scientists there were also getting ready to ride the coming wave of everything that would happen with digital photography, and later when video cameras met mobile phones. Together with microcontrollers for embedded applications, the resulting business would be massive.

Instead in Agrate, Catania, and Castelletto, the new SGS-ATES was exploring avenues for growth in the field of power devices. In some sense, it was a decisive moment. Italy was at a crossroads that, greatly simplified, led in two directions: digital or analog.

"In light of our competencies, we opted for analog," explains Murari, reflecting on that time. "Electronics is replete with technologies that have to factor in high voltage, high current, bugs, interference, temperature. Power devices never have 100 percent yield; they have to dissipate energy. So you have to consider the mechanical aspects, the materials you use, the packaging. We concentrated on this area, which is analog in many ways, and we did it starting from a very specific field: amplification."

"When Fairchild left us on our own," adds Romano, who worked with Murari at that time, "a new era began for us and our company. We had to stand on our own two feet, and move forward alone because there were no longer technologies from other companies to produce. We developed the first integrated circuits – completely designed and manufactured in Europe – without an American license. They were devices for radios and televisions. The problem was that the European market was small. We mainly went to Germany to sell to Grundig, Blaupunkt and others. But that wasn't enough to fill our production capacity."

It's true that from an economic standpoint the numbers didn't add up and the balance sheet stayed in the red. But as far as creativity and marketing, it was a time of important lessons that would prove useful later on. The first was knowing how to listen to customers and work with them to make products specifically for a single application (one that they knew inside out) or a customized product.

The biggest problem was still market growth. Already back in the early 1970s, despite the weaknesses and limitations SGS-ATES was contending with, the company attempted an incursion into the most important market of all: the US.

"Around 1972, we opened an office in Boston," recalls Romano, "and we put an Italian manager in charge, Pietro Fox, and his wife, who worked as his secretary. The two of them were supposed to conquer America. Our initial strategy was to focus on price, marketing standard devices that local industry needed and offering them for a penny less than American suppliers. But it didn't work. We were an unknown entity and competitive pricing wasn't enough. No one seemed to want to entrust Italians with semiconductor production in a country full of big names in the industry. We were about to give up and shut Boston down when we tried a new strategy promoting innovative products. That helped us win our first customer. It was Zenith, one of the pioneers of color TV at the time. They bought two of our products, which became components in their TV production assembly lines."

Although it was a crucial first step in breaking into the US market, it was certainly not enough to change the bottom line. SGS-ATES were having a hard time coming up with a sustainable business model. But at the same time, the talented people at the company were learning methods and lessons that would soon prove to be invaluable. And the same thing was also happening in France at Thomson.

Carlo Bozotti, the former CEO of STMicroelectronics who joined the company in 1977, provides us with a snapshot of that era.

"When I arrived, SGS-ATES' turnover was the equivalent of €60 million in today's euros. The company's business units were organized by type of technology, for example, discrete power and linear integrated circuits. Then for each unit there were the different functions, so there was R&D, there was production, and then there were the product managers who essentially handled strategy, application development and technical promotion. They were applications for the consumer market, mainly for television. Examples of products were power transistors for the power supply for TVs, or for horizontal cathode ray deflection. Then there were products for what today is known as 'car infotainment', but we simply called car radios back then. The other areas we were breaking into – or trying to break into – were industrial production, automotive and then telecommunications."

In the early 1980s, turnover hit €100 million (of which the US market accounted for €10 million), but behind these numbers was hiding a business teetering on the brink. SGS had been in the red since the semiconductor crisis of 1970 and remained in debt throughout the decade. At some plants in Europe, for example Sweden and Germany, work stoppages were routine. In Agrate, the company had to lay off workers and resort to government payroll subsidies on more than one occasion. As the 1980s began, the company was essentially bankrupt and only stayed afloat thanks to the very Italian mechanism of "loss compensation." At the end of the year, the company CEO went to IRI headquarters in Rome and was handed a check for the exact amount – right down to the lira – to cover the losses incurred in the year.

The state was propping up the semiconductor industry in both Italy and France, despite the fact that both countries were home to companies with enormous potential, enormous talent, and any number of products that could stand up to the competition. It was time for a shakeup. Italy was the first to make the move. Then France took its turn, and completed the process of aggregating its complex semiconductor ecosystem. Everything was being prepped on both sides of the Alps for the birth of Silicon Europe.

What was missing, as the major players of the time realized, was one essential ingredient. The state-sponsored approach that both countries had followed up till then wouldn't work in a market that was going global. If the US was too far ahead to catch up with on digital innovation, a dose of the American approach to business was probably what it would take to turn Italian and French companies around and make them competitive.

"What made the difference was introducing the American management style in SGS and Thomson," explains Alain Dutheil, the Chief Operating Officer of STMicroelectronics for many years, and a manager who got his training at the big US semiconductor companies. He joined Texas Instruments in 1969 and climbed the corporate ladder all through the 1970s. His boss at the American company was another Frenchman, Jacques Noels, who in the early 1980s was asked to head the newly formed Thomson Semiconducteurs in France. Dutheil joined him, along with other managers from Motorola, Texas Instruments, and Intel. "We brought a different approach to the company," says Dutheil, "and American DNA, which no doubt is what Thomson desperately needed, because the situation inside the company was a disaster."

It was coming full circle. After going to learn the secrets of transistors in America and then working in large US companies, it was time to go from brain drain to brain gain. Silicon Europe was about to get a new lease of life, tapping into the skills gained across the pond. "They called us 'cowboys,'" says Dutheil, "and the first things we did created a lot of friction. But it was the right cure." The impact that the Silicon Cowboys had in France was powerful, but it was nothing compared to what happened in Italy at the hands of a man who was completely unconventional.

An "American" – born in Sicily.

8 The Sicilian from Arizona

Headhunters

As the 1980s began, the whole of the electronic components industry in Europe was hemorrhaging money and the situation was looking hopeless. The field of semiconductors was clustered in small domestic markets, and mainly concentrated on producing devices for television and radio. It didn't appear to have the power to move – or the ability to see – beyond national borders. Globalization was coming to bear, and businesses could go to other countries to set up production and take a stab at competing on the international market, but European companies through the decade prior lacked the skills and the economic prerequisites to do so. One of Motorola's top American executives described what he pictured of the situation at the time like this (exaggerating somewhat): "Europe is lagging behind America by months in terms of semiconductor technology, by years in terms of manufacturing, and by decades in terms of marketing."[1]

In France, the state was trying to bridge this gap by promoting scientific research and investing in the military sector, but the Grenoble and Provence hubs could not reach the necessary critical mass to break out of the French market. In Italy the situation was even worse, aggravated by tensions with trade unions and fears of terrorism, impacting factories and discouraging potential foreign partners from in-

---

[1] Giovanni Russo, *Il futuro è a Catania* [The Future is in Catania], Milan, Sperling & Kupfer, 1997, p. 7.

vesting on Italian soil. SGS-ATES was a leading light, but it couldn't shine beyond national borders. Then, right when this dismal state of affairs seemed to be devolving toward the worst possible outcome, STET played the right card, galvanizing a turnaround that seemed unimaginable.

The opportunity came in 1980, when sadly the then CEO of SGS-ATES was battling a serious illness. The parent company STET needed to find a replacement and delegated the task to Boyden, a headhunting firm. STET outlined a few specific job requirements that seemed too restrictive, but in the end proved to be prophetic. The new CEO had to be Italian, decided STET. But since America represented the dominant market in the sector, the candidate had to be living and working in the US at a large American semiconductor company, and currently holding an executive management position, which would allow him or her to take the helm of a company the size of SGS-ATES.

Boyden scoured the market and discovered that there were only two people who fit the bill. One was Federico Faggin, but convincing him to move to SGS-ATES would be an impossible feat. The Italian physicist and manager had left Intel in 1974 and founded his own company in Silicon Valley called Zilog. His new venture was making its fortune on 8-bit microprocessors, the Z80 Series, which were Intel-8080 compatible and very price competitive. As Boyden was scouting for candidates, Zilog was in talks with Exxon on a takeover, and it was unlikely that Faggin would be persuaded to give up everything to run a state-controlled Italian company that was deep in debt.

The other candidate was in Phoenix, Arizona, and he was perfect for the job. An excellent manager with a reputation for knowing how to handle human resources too. A Sicilian "transplanted" in America, and destined to make his mark on the history of European electronics. His name was Pasquale Pistorio. His career path, which had taken him to Arizona, reflected the international experience he had accrued up until that spring of 1980, when STET went looking for him.

"I was born in 1936 in Agira, an ancient village in the heart of Sicily, in the province of Enna," the octogenarian Pistorio tells us. Sitting in the meeting room of a building in the center of Milan, for hours we've been poring over the history of Silicon Europe, and he never forgets a name, a date, or a financial result. His friendly smile and sparkling eyes haven't changed since the 1980s. The moustache has turned silver, and it's not as thick as it was in the photos from back then, but it's still a mark of distinction. Even the dark pinstripe suit and tie exudes an impeccable twentieth-century elegance.

Pistorio grew up in a family of small landowners, but though they once enjoyed a comfortable quality of life, they eventually fell on hard times. His grandfather Pasquale (our protagonist's namesake) owned a horse stable and some land, but sold it all to start trading in wheat, olive oil and almonds. Business was good for a while, but then World War II broke out. Troubles began and bankruptcy ensued, so Pasquale's father had to support the family. "My father worked for the farmers' cooperative till the day he died, and he sacrificed a great deal to send my brother and me to school," Pistorio recalls. But a commercial and entrepreneurial spirit was clearly encoded in the family's DNA.

> "I spent my adolescence in Catania, which compared to Agira was already another world," Pistorio recalls. "I came from a small town where my father had won my mother over with meaningful glances and penetrating looks, as he rode back and forth on horseback under her balcony. In Catania I went to live in a widow's house. I did all my high school there, and went back to Agira three times a year to help my father when it was time to sell the wheat."

Given his excellent grades, Pistorio's high school teachers urged him to go on to study engineering. But in Sicily, that was not an option. Anyone on the island who had this ambition usually ended up in a completely different part of the country, at what was then Italy's most prestigious engineering university: the Turin Polytechnic, the alma mater of Galileo Ferraris and Camillo Olivetti. In Turin, Pistorio shared an apartment with two of his high school classmates. (One of them was Salvatore Castorina, who would go on to become an ST manager too.) They had no heating, which meant in winter the water pipe for the shower would freeze, so they had to put it over the burner on the gas stove to thaw it out. In 1963, Pistorio finished his degree in electronic engineering, specializing in "weak currents." Translation: semiconductors.

"Back in the day, when you graduated in engineering, you were guaranteed a job. Companies would come looking for you," Pistorio recalls. For him it was Olivetti, which was at the forefront of the semiconductor industry via Floriani's SGS and Fairchild back then. But the time was not yet ripe for Pistorio and SGS to unite, and that was probably lucky for both parties. It was Metroelettronica's agent in Turin who reached out to Pistorio and convinced him to turn down Olivetti and go to work for that company, the Motorola distributor for Italy, instead.

At the time, the American company was a consolidated colossus. Founded in 1928 by Paul Galvin as the Galvin Manufacturing Corporation and shortly after that renamed Motorola, it was a world leader in telecommunications. In the 1960s, like many other American companies, Motorola ventured into semiconductors, but maintained its role as front-runner in radio communications. Indeed, when Neil Armstrong uttered those famous words as he stepped foot on the moon in 1969 ("That's one small step for man, one giant leap for mankind"), he was speaking into a Motorola device.

"They offered me a position in sales for Motorola," Pistorio continues, "and at first I told them that it wasn't my job; I had a degree in engineering and Olivetti wanted to hire me. But then they convinced me and I accepted, partly because they offered me 150,000 lire a month, compared to 125,000 from Olivetti. I began to work as a Motorola distributor, first in Turin and Piedmont, then – since selling came easy to me, maybe also thanks to the family tradition – I became a sales manager in Milan. A short time later, Motorola decided not to use distributors anymore, but to open their own office in Milan instead. They sent an American, who became the CEO of Motorola Italy, but actually it was the two of us and two secretaries, and I oversaw all Italian sales. It was a young industry, but there was explosive growth in semiconductors. I immediately fell in love with the work and I did my job well."

To America and back again

In just a few years, Pistorio's career took off. First, he was sent to Motorola's European headquarters in Geneva in the role of Sales Manager for Europe. In time, he became General Manager, overseeing all of the company's European business. Finally, in 1977, Motorola decided to promote him again and bring him to the US, to the semiconductor headquarters in Phoenix, Arizona. Here his job title was World Director of Marketing. Pistorio's sphere of action became the entire globe (excluding the US market), and soon after that he was also appointed Vice President.

"I was the first non-American corporate vice president at the company," Pistorio remembers, "And for my wife and me those were wonderful years, very intense. We had a beautiful home in Phoenix and the company gave executives special treatment. I remember once the big boss, Bob Galvin, the son of the founder, invited us along with some other vice presidents to his home in Chicago for a little party. He came up to my wife, he had never seen her before, and told her: 'Lisa, I know the move to Arizona was really difficult for you, and that you did it for your husband, who is an excellent corporate vice president. I want to thank you for that.' She was deeply touched by what he did. Bob Galvin was a true gentleman."

Galvin was also a great manager who stood at the helm of Motorola from 1959 to 1986. Beyond developing the group's worldwide network, he was also an innovator when it came to work organization. He personally guided the process that led to the Six Sigma quality control system, a model developed at Motorola that many other companies have adopted over the years and is still popular today.

A work environment such as the one Galvin created was undoubtedly very different from what could be found anywhere in Europe at the time, to include the factories of SGS-ATES and Thomson. Motorola's production models were similar to the kind that Jacques Noels and Alain Dutheil were trying out at Texas Instruments, which they would later take back to France. However, the Italian STET preempted Thomson, and sought out Pistorio, convinced that a manager with his background was just the ticket for relaunching Agrate, Catania, and the other production centers.

"When they made me the offer," Pistorio recalls, "I burst out laughing. I said: 'Sorry gentlemen, but I'm doing very well here and from what I've

heard SGS-ATES is in serious trouble.' But there were two things that
made me think it over and leave the door open. The first was that they
offered me the post of CEO of the company, and that was my career
goal. In Motorola's semiconductor branch I might have gotten there one
day, but who knows when. The other thing was that my parents and
in-laws were getting older and they were starting to need our help. The
head of personnel at STET, Mr. Silvestri, would phone me every other
day to try and convince me to at least come and visit the plants in Italy.
I knew that SGS-ATES had been on the brink of bankruptcy for ten
years, and only later I found out that it was only scraping along thanks
to loss compensation from IRI. There were some strengths – such as
the research that Murari and Zocchi, the head of Agrate's R&D, were
doing, and Romano's department – and there were some good products
too. But the situation looked pretty hopeless."

But they kept the lines of communication open, and when the position of CEO became vacant, STET turned up the pressure on Pistorio. There weren't many arguments to use to win him over, least of all
economic considerations.

"The most they could offer to pay me was 80 million lire. They couldn't
give me more because that was the salary of the president of IRI. But at
the time I was earning $150,000 a year, which was more or less 150 mil-
lion lire, plus a performance bonus, which was around 20 percent to 40
percent a year, plus stock options. Frankly, it was a huge financial sacri-
fice. But in the end what convinced me was the challenge, the desire to
be CEO and to return to Italy, and also the encouragement of my wife."

In Phoenix, they couldn't believe it. Pistorio had just achieved a tremendous success. He had launched a global marketing campaign
with the slogan: "It's time." This was the battle cry that rallied the
company to successfully usurp Texas Instruments and take over as
number one in the world in semiconductors.

"I remember the meeting I had with John Welty, my boss in Phoenix,
when I went to tell him that I was leaving the company to go to SGS-
ATES," Pistorio tells us. "He looked at me with a puzzled expression as
he smoked his pipe. 'Well, Pasquale, I see. But tell me this: SGS, is it
a big company?' 'No John, it's practically bankrupt.' 'Ah, I see. And tell
me: Is Italy a nice place to work?' 'No, John, not right now. There are the

Red Brigades who kill business managers every week.' 'Ah, I see. And tell me: Are they paying you more than Motorola?' 'No, John, they'll pay me less than half.' He looked me straight in the eye, taking a long pull from his pipe, puffed out the smoke and then asked me: 'Pasquale, have you lost your mind?' 'Yes, John, I think I have.'"

"Indeed, returning to Italy was a shock in many ways," Pistorio continues. "Our lifestyle was turned upside down after so many years in Geneva and Phoenix. But as far as the work, it was a really exciting challenge: taking a failing company and turning it around, breathing new life into it. The task motivated me enormously."

The Pistorios took their time returning to Italy – on the first (and only) cruise of their lives. They sailed from Boston to Plymouth, and during the eight days of navigation the manager studied all the documents that STET had given him to get a clear grasp of the situation at SGS. From Plymouth they continued on to London, and from there flew to Milan. The welcoming committee at Linate Airport consisted of Luigi Bonavoglia, chairman of the board at SGS-ATES, and Domenico Faro, general manager of STET; together the two managers accompanied Pistorio directly to Agrate for his first meeting with the company's executives.

"That was just a chance to shake hands and get to know a few names," Pistorio recalls. "But first thing the next morning I called all my colleagues together and explained that I wanted to have an hour-long face-to-face meeting with each of them and that they should come prepared to answer three questions: What do you do? What are the strengths/weaknesses of the company? What advice would you give me? There were 100 managers and I met them all, day after day, from 7 in the morning to 10 at night. By the end of the interviews, there were 80 managers left. I fired 20 in that first month. Because I was a bad guy? No, because I felt that what they were doing was not necessary, or that they were not the right people. There was one person who was put there by STET just to keep his ears open and report back – he told me that his job was to welcome STET guests and organize their stays. Another one, the marketing manager, told me that the products were worthless: 'It's a miracle we're still taking orders from a couple of customers.' I told him, 'And you, as marketing director, travel around the world with that attitude?'"

It was immediately clear to everyone that there was change in the air. Now there was a CEO who was at his desk from 7 am to 10 pm. And in one month, he'd already fired one manager out of five.

"The second month I set out to tackle absenteeism," says Pistorio. "I knew that the average was 17 percent: every day 17 people out of 100 didn't come to work, and they had no justification. That was inconceivable to me. At Motorola, absenteeism was less than 3 percent, and if it hit 4 percent, emergency measures were automatically activated. I asked the head of HR to check for any people who had been absent 50 percent of the time or more for a three-year period. He found 17, and I told him to fire them immediately. He looked at me with a polite smile: 'Sir, in Italy you can fire managers, but not clerks or factory workers.' I replied: 'Sir, I didn't ask you whether we can fire them, I told you to fire them.' We found a rider in the Workers' Charter that allowed us to do so and the layoffs started. All hell broke loose. Every morning the driver would drop me off at the gates in Agrate and I'd walk through a crowd hurling insults at me."

The leader of the workers' protest challenged Pistorio to a one-on-one confrontation, but as an affront, refused to meet in the CEO's office. So instead, they met at the union leader's home, where Pistorio was greeted by the union leader himself, his wife, and their children. "We had a frank discussion, and I explained why we couldn't defend 17 people and their serial absenteeism, because we would be putting the jobs of thousands of other employees at risk. The next day, the protesters removed their picket lines, our activities resumed and absenteeism plummeted to less than 4 percent."

But in 1980s Italy, the head of a company who did what Pistorio had done in two months wasn't just risking protests from the union. One day, after the *Brigate Rosse* (Red Brigades) attacked yet another business manager, someone called the SGS switchboard and simply said: "Pistorio is next." A few days later, someone shot machine gun rounds at the walls of the company headquarters that overlook the Milan–Venice highway.

"A group of well-dressed men came to my office," Pistorio recalls. "And they explained to me that the threats were no longer ambiguous. In a hideout of the Red Brigades, they found my name on a hit list. The men told me: 'From now on, you need to put bullet-proof doors in your office. And you must wear a bullet-proof vest at all times, even when you go to the canteen. Lastly, buy two guns. Keep one in your belt, behind your back, and keep the other one in your shoulder bag. And learn how to shoot. We'll give you a bodyguard who will serve as a driver and if for any reason they stop your car, lower your window and shoot; you'll scare them off.' My wife Lisa saw the new procedures being implemented, of course, including our bodyguard-driver. Whenever I got home he would check the stairs [of our building] before letting me get out of the car. She was very worried. I tried to calm her down: 'It's nothing, don't worry about it. It's just that they're paranoid at STET, and they've set up these procedures for all the chief executives, otherwise they fire us. Do want to get me fired?' It was a difficult period, but thank God nothing happened to us."

Despite the challenges and dangers, Pistorio immediately set out to reorganize production and restructure the company.

"I studied all our strengths – especially bipolar technologies and intelligent power modules – and organized everything by product groups and geographical regions. I also brought some people in from Motorola. But most importantly I sought to make the most of the high-profile managers who already worked here. I have a theory of leadership that I've always used in my professional life; I immediately put it to the test at SGS. As I see it, a leader has to do five things. First: Create the vision. Second: Build the team. Third: Instill a corporate culture. Fourth: Draw the roadmap. Fifth: Drive execution. I applied these simple concepts, which to me are as relevant for a manager as they are for a mayor. We set to work with the aim of turning things around as quickly as possible, because a company cannot live in the red."

The "Pistorio Cure" took a couple of years of hard work to make a total about-face before the first positive outcomes appeared. June 1982 was the first month in many years that SGS actually closed in the black. The management team celebrated in a trattoria in Agrate with sandwiches and wine, to maintain the thrifty, cost-cutting approach adopted in those years. The first year that the company turned a profit in more than a decade was 1983, "and since then and for all the years I was at the helm of the company," Pistorio recalls, "we always closed with a profit."

Vision 2000

In Catania, Pistorio sparked a revolution in the old ATES plant. "It was a factory that was completely dilapidated, but it did have potential," recalls the manager. To run it he chose another Sicilian, his old roommate in Turin, Salvatore Castorina, who showed up and implemented initiatives that ended up creating the same kind of problems that Pistorio had faced in Agrate.

> "Our production required night shifts too," Pistorio explains, "and in the semiconductor industry, a large proportion of the workforce has always been made up of women. Castorina decided that night shifts couldn't be staffed just by the men, so he set them up for women too. We were the first Italian company to do anything like it, and in Catania no less, where the local culture made it even more problematic. It was a revolution that unleashed protests – it was seen as an American thing. The workers would go and sing songs like '*Tu vuò fa l'americano*' under the balcony of Castorina's house,[2] or shout at him, '*La notte è fatta per amare, te lo sei dimenticato solo tu*' ('The night is made for love, only you have forgotten that'), which for a Sicilian is a serious insult. But the idea of women working night shifts was eventually accepted, in Catania and in Agrate, and became a way to reinforce the company, and to save jobs too."

Catania was destined to become one of the great success stories of STMicroelectronics, but at the time it seemed fated to lag behind in the fast-paced world of semiconductors. Carmelo Papa, who would become head of one of the main ST product groups, still remembers the day in 1982 when he happened to be passing through Catania, and he went to visit a friend in the SGS-ATES plant. Papa was a native of Catania, but after graduating in physics he left Sicily and

---

[2] A famous Neapolitan song by Renato Carosone; the words loosely translate as "You're trying to act like an American."

entered the world of computers in Germany and Great Britain. This
is how he describes the scene:

> "It seemed like a world of madmen, completely different from the rest of
> the city. It was a factory with people from all different backgrounds, an
> English marketing manager, very little discipline but a lot of imagina-
> tion and enthusiasm. I was impressed, intrigued.
> "A year later there was a job listing in the newspapers for a position in
> Catania, and Castorina was asking: 'Do you want to come and work for
> us? We can offer you blood and tears.' I liked the idea. I had just inter-
> viewed at Olivetti, I wanted to come back to Italy to work, and they had
> sent me the letter of employment. I surprised both Olivetti and my wife
> and chose SGS-ATES instead. I went to Catania with the intention of
> staying there for two years at most. I ended up staying for 16, heading
> up the company's marketing department."

In Catania there was a deep pool of skills and expertise that had not
yet been tapped. To foster it, Papa started from the work culture (as
Pistorio and Castorina had done before him), where attitudes needed
to change.

> "I came from countries where discipline was the rule of the day; when
> you organized a meeting, nobody was late. I started scheduling meetings
> at nine o'clock in the morning. The first few times, some people arrived
> five minutes late, others a little later. So I started locking the door at
> nine o'clock and taking the names of the people who were there and the
> ones who hadn't arrived yet. I became the terror of my group. But in no
> time, they got the picture."

Little details, but they sent the message that things were changing,
and all this at a time when surviving and becoming profitable again
meant reorganizing.

At SGS-ATES (which changed its name to SGS Microelettronica), Pistorio wanted to put some order into the entire ecosystem before trying to break into international markets. He did this by picking
out the key people at each plant, and then going to visit them all in
person. After the Italian plants, it was time to go to Asia. Zargani
hadn't stopped in Singapore, but expanded the presence of SGS to

neighboring Malaysia, opening one of his temporary factories in the middle of an actual jungle, in the village of Muar. As Zargani remembers it: "We started production there in the huts abandoned by the Japanese after the Second World War. There was nothing else in Muar, so we built everything ourselves."

When Pistorio visited Muar, for some time Zargani had been busy setting up plants in other places around the globe, and the factory was nothing like today's state-of-the-art facility in the Malaysian city. "I was quite shocked," says Pistorio, "because I arrived during the lunch break and saw the workers eating outside, in all that humidity. They were under a tarp, and flies were everywhere. I told the local managers that I would be back soon and I wanted to find a clean, air-conditioned, indoor canteen." Today, Muar is one of the most efficient semiconductor factories in the world, and STMicroelectronics' Muar-Singapore system is an integrated Asian hub, with a staff of around 5,000 handling the design, production, and distribution of high technology.

> "We were among the first to take a gamble on Singapore and to take production there, instead of seeing it just as an assembly hub," Pistorio says. "At the time it was considered a low-cost location. It wasn't the efficient city it is today, with its research centers and the excellent engineering school at the university. But we believed in it from the beginning, and I am very proud to have been conferred honorary citizenship. I believe I was the first honorary citizen in Singapore's history."

Pistorio chose a model with a strategic approach that the former manager describes as "globalization through an integrated presence in each major macroeconomic system." In practice, this meant that to compete on a global scale, SGS had to have marketing, design, and manufacturing in Europe (where a plant had also been set up in Malta), in Asia (Singapore-Muar, in addition to China some time later), and in America (where a second factory for front-end semiconductor manufacturing had been opened).

To be successful on the other side of the pond, SGS needed to scale up, there was no doubt about that. The global market, especially the American one, was out of reach for a company of its size.

But what wasn't lacking in the Italian company and its CEO was
vision and ambition. In 1983, Pistorio launched a new strategy
– Vision 2000 – with three goals to achieve before the new millennium began: to transform the company into one of the world's
top ten semiconductor manufacturers; to out-earn the world's top
ten companies in profits, on average; and to be recognized as a
leader in corporate social responsibility and environmental sustainability.

"It sounds impossible, but we succeeded before 2000. In fact, back
in 1997, we had already met all these targets," Pistorio explains.

And the road to this success led through France.

The Gomez Cure

Pistorio had been working at SGS for just under a year when a wa-
tershed moment occurred in France that would have critical consequences for Silicon Europe. In May 1981, François Mitterrand was
elected to lead the country, and the president entrusted his campaign
spokesman, Pierre Mauroy, with the task of assembling a socialist
government. One of the most significant initiatives undertaken by
Mauroy's left-wing government was to nationalize five of France's
major industrial groups – including Thomson S.A.

The company had turned into a shambolic conglomerate that
lacked focus on any specific business. Thomson started out as a manufacturer of household appliances (from washing machines to fridg-
es), but over the years had tossed lots of other items into its corporate
portfolio. There was a sizeable production of military equipment for
the Armed Forces, which was the main reason why Thomson was
strategic for the government. There was a growing specialization in
consumer electronics, particularly radios, TVs, and audio recording
devices. And there was the whole semiconductor branch that was
intertwined with the other sectors that produced basic devices but
failed to scale up and grow globally.

The French government was facing challenges not unlike those
IRI and the Italian governments were contending with. The question
was what to do with high-tech industries that were perpetually hem-

orrhaging money and incapable of competing in international markets. The Thomson conglomerate was on the verge of bankruptcy when the government decided to nationalize it and tapped Alain Gomez to take the helm. This Harvard-educated manager had risen up through the internal hierarchy of another French giant Saint-Gobain.

The cure Gomez prescribed was a drastic one: slashing expenses, imposing new American-style management systems, and reorganizing. As a sign of the break from the past, the old headquarters were transferred from an elegant Parisian building on Boulevard Haussmann to a modern office building in La Défense. The most critical move of all was when Gomez brought in a new generation of managers, most in their thirties, who had trained in other corporate contexts.[3]

One of these young managers was Jacques Noels, the head of Texas Instruments in France, who was tasked with leading the newly founded Thomson Semiconducteurs.

> "Jacques was facing similar challenges as Pasquale in Italy at the time," recollects Alain Dutheil, who also worked at Texas Instruments. "He looked around and realized that he needed people who really knew semiconductors, because at Thomson they were doing lots of different things, but often to the detriment of specialization. That's why Jacques came looking for me: 'I'm trying to build a new industry in France, because a real semiconductor industry doesn't actually exist: if you want to join me, you're welcome.' So I went, and several other managers from American companies came with me."

Now the "cowboys" (as some scornfully called them) were running the rodeo. It was a time with many striking parallels to what was happening in Italy with SGS-ATES – first and foremost, the need to transform the corporate culture.

> "The first job Jacques gave me was to run the production center we had in Aix-en-Provence," Dutheil explains. "He asked me to figure out what to do with it and I quickly realized that the only thing to do was to shut it down, keeping on the excellent engineers we had but transferring

---

[3] Janice McCormick and Nan Stone, "From National Champion to Global Competitor: An Interview with Thomson's Alain Gomez," *Harvard Business Review* (May–June 1990).

them elsewhere. The first day I arrived in Aix I asked to see the production reports and the financial results. It was May and they still only had the previous year's reports. I had come from an American company where you saw and discussed the numbers month by month, and that was crucial in an industry like semiconductors, where change happened fast. But the French industrial approach at that time was 'don't make a fuss.' Certainly, introducing an American approach came as a shock, but a necessary one."

Meanwhile, Gomez was acting with determination to position Thomson as a leader in the global TV sector. He was also setting his sights on companies in crisis with the aim of reaching global dimensions via acquisitions. As a result, a number of European competitors entered Thomson's orbit, such as Telefunken and Saba from Germany and Ferguson from the UK. But on the semiconductor front, the only path to growth led through the American market, the most lucrative in the world at the time. So, Thomson launched a daring operation: the acquisition of Mostek.

The history of semiconductors, and electronics as a whole, is replete with companies that were founded by "runaways" from other companies. Case in point: Fairchild, founded by defectors from Shockley; or Intel, by managers who had decamped from Fairchild. In the case of Mostek, it was former Texas Instruments employees who created the company in 1969. By the 1970s, Mostek had grown into a major presence in the field of integrated circuits. At the Carrollton plant in Texas, they specialized in DRAM (dynamic random-access memory) chips, which were fundamental components at a time when the market for personal computers and software was exploding. New players were arriving on the market in droves, and they needed microprocessors and memory to run their innovative computers, which were starting to pop up not only in offices, but also in homes too. These computers had names that became famous overnight: IBM PC, Macintosh, Commodore 64, Amiga, Atari, and Sinclair.

Mostek had built a reputation for reliability in semiconductors, and the company was producing chips for (and under license from) Intel, Fairchild, and Faggin's Zilog. But it bet too heavily on volatile memory at a time when the market was becoming extremely competitive. Volatile memory was the designated battle ground of the Japanese, who were followed by the Koreans at Samsung. The two swiftly conquered the entire segment thanks in part to their competitive labor markets. Mostek's key customer for DRAM was IBM, which unexpectedly decided to switch suppliers and turned to Japan's Toshiba, which had drastically slashed its prices. In a matter of weeks, Mostek virtually collapsed and had to put its assets up for sale.

Enter Thomson, who caught a whiff of the opportunity to make a splash on the American market. Between Christmas and New Year's Eve 1985, the French government gave Gomez and Noels the go-ahead to acquire what remained of Mostek. Now it was time to go to Texas, to get the plant up and running again and decide what to do with it. Noels tapped 30-year-old Joel Hartmann.

> "I was working at LETI in Grenoble back then," as Hartmann tells it. "I had joined in the late 1970s as a young engineering student doing my PhD. When Mostek collapsed, we were shocked, because it was a high-profile company that had made a huge mistake, and we learned from it. They thought IBM would be their forever client, and had no worries about the future. When they went bankrupt, they had to shut down the Carrollton plant and lay off their workers. They only kept on three or four hundred that they could call up if they somehow managed to resume production."

Hartmann and his colleagues at LETI had worked in close collaboration with Thomson, in particular through EFCIS. They were very familiar with the Carrollton operations, where they were working on 1.2-micron CMOS integrated circuits[4] and DRAM processes. The French labs in Grenoble were in the process of developing these same technologies.

> "What we proposed was to blend our activities with what they were doing in Texas, and I raised my hand to volunteer to go to Carrollton," Hartmann recollects. "It was a great experience and a total shock. When I got there, they treated me with enormous respect, because there was an entire town in Texas that lived off of Mostek and they were all out

---

[4] We'll take a closer look at the characteristics of CMOS in Chapter 10.

of work. I found enormous gratitude for the French government and for Thomson, and I also found a factory that was totally abandoned, a phantom factory; it looked like everyone had escaped from a fire. We got to work and got it going again."

With the acquisition of Mostek and the reorganization of several semiconductor activities at Thomson (including the purchase of the Eurotechnique plant in Rousset), a long journey was finished. It had led from the chaos of the 1960s to the rise of a strong French national player in the sector. "In the 1970s we were really bad at semiconductors," Gomez later explained. "We messed everything up and missed every opportunity. We got better as we gained experience, but we were still too small. We still didn't have enough market share to compete, not even on the European market."[5]

Thomson had specialized in all things MOS, transistors that were essential ingredients in manufacturing microchips for the digital industry that was emerging. On the other side of the Alps, in contrast SGS-ATES had established robust production in power transistors and analog integrated circuits. They were two complementary companies controlled by their respective governments that, when combined, would create a Silicon Europe colossus. It was clear that the performance of professional electronic systems would be increasingly contingent on the integration of innovative semiconductors, which required the use of multiple silicon technologies. An annual R&D allotment of hundreds of millions of dollars would be needed, and the only companies that could afford it were the ones that reached critical mass, which meant 3 percent of the world semiconductor market.

In Milan, Rome, Paris, and Grenoble, they started seriously thinking about it.

The joint venture

"I met Jacques Noels back when he was at Texas Instruments and I was at Motorola," recalls Pistorio, "and in 1984 we started discussing our respective new assignments. We got together at meetings organized by

---

[5] McCormick and Stone, "Interview with Alain Gomez."

JESSI (Joint European Submicron Silicon Initiative), a European initiative for the coordination and development of the semiconductor industry. All the European companies at that time were in the red, SGS was the only one that was back in the black. Thomson hadn't had time yet, it still needed to turn around. I started toying with the idea with Noels. 'Jacques,' I said, 'our companies are too small, we don't have the scale to compete in the world. How about a merger?'"

The time was ripe. The right people were in the right place leading the companies; the semiconductor industry was in the throes of another cyclical crises (chip boom in 1984, market crash in 1985), so it was unavoidable to think seriously about size. The meetings became more frequent; the idea took shape. Pistorio went to see Thomson's facilities, and Noels returned the visit by going to Agrate.

"In the end," recalls the Italian manager, "we presented our proposal to the respective shareholders: we wanted a merger between equals. At STET they weren't on board right away, but Alain Gomez was much more open to the idea. SGS at that time was the smallest semiconductor company in Europe, but it was more or less the same size as Thomson Semiconducteurs. In 1987, the key year of the merger, sales at both companies were around $400 million. Thomson had no debt because it was actually a division, so its debts were held by its parent company. We were drowning in debt, about $350 million, and they were drowning in losses, about $200 million out of $400 million in turnover. Taken together, the two companies would have faced an avalanche of debts and losses, and the shareholders were skeptical, to say the least. 'What are you thinking?' they asked. 'That two dead bodies are better than one? Besides, in Europe there is no job mobility, you can't fire people, you'd have to close a lot of factories.' But we knew that the two companies were complementary, and we really had faith in the deal."

There were other key players who believed in the merger too. One was Gomez, who pushed hard to overcome the resistance of the French government. The other was an economist who had been put in charge of IRI in 1982 by the government of Giovanni Spadolini, and who would go on to hold many other posts, including Prime Minister in Italy and President of the European Commission in Brussels.

To understand that transition in the 1980s, and the impact it had on Silicon Europe, we need to go to Bologna. In the historical heart of the city, we find the headquarters of the Foundation for Collaboration between Peoples, and walk into the office of its president: Romano Prodi. We see a stack of open files on the table of the president of IRI; it was a time of deep reorganizations and critical privatizations – such as that of Alfa Romeo, completed in 1986. One of the files is on the merger between SGS Microelettronica and Thomson, and Prodi remembers well what top management at STET was saying at the time.

> "STET for me was, among the IRI subsidiaries, the one with the most astute leaders," he says, "and they had done a technical analysis that convinced us that there could be advantages to merging with the French. Since we were in trouble and so were they, it made sense to create something together. Knowing the French, I think that such a thing never would have happened unless it was an absolute necessity. That's why the merger took place and it went well."

A key ingredient in the success of the merger, according to Prodi, was Pistorio.

> "I'd heard good things about him back when they told me that there was an Italian willing to come back from America to take over SGS," says Prodi. "They said he was a top expert in semiconductors, and a highly intelligent person. The first time we met (the first of many meetings), he came up to me with his curious accent and a large briefcase. He opened it, took out his papers and said: 'Dear President, I think you are obviously very ignorant about [semiconductors]' (He was right!) and proceeded to explain it to me. Pistorio was a team builder, an energizer, and he was technically competent too, which was also why the French accepted him as the boss."

One of the concerns circulating on the Italian side of the negotiations was that the company would ultimately be under the control of the French. It was supposed to be an operation between equals, but in Rome there were preconceived opinions (fueled by some past history) about whether Paris was truly willing to accept a 50–50 agreement. "Our issue," as Prodi explains, "was the initial question we had: 'What are we doing, a joint venture with the French who will devour us?' There were internal debates on this, but actually there were no problems, and everyone also accepted that it was Pistorio who was in charge of everything."

Prodi's admiration for Pistorio had been growing over the years, even before the merger, whenever the manager came to report to the president of IRI on developments in the sector, innovations, and profits, at a time when the public conglomerate was chock full of companies that were running at a loss.

> "I was particularly impressed with what was going on in Catania, which I kept very close tabs on," Prodi recollects. "There were skilled engineers there who were doing great things. Pistorio told me that as far as recruiting personnel, there was no better place than Catania, but the problem was that people didn't want to leave to go to Agrate or anywhere else."

In Prodi's view, the merger with the French was truly a European project, a step toward creating a champion in the sector for the continent. He was tremendously satisfied with the successful Italian–French merger, in part because there had been no guarantee it would happen considering the enormous challenges involved. "If it hadn't been for this joint venture, it would probably have been the end of the chip industry in Italy. It could have gone badly, like it went badly for Olivetti, where they had no one to champion the cause, and they didn't get behind the transition from mechanics to electronics with the same enthusiasm. What shocked me about Olivetti was how fast it collapsed. With SGS and Thomson, instead, it was a marriage of equals, and luckily the shareholders saw eye to eye on the mutual benefits of the deal."

On April 29, 1987, the merger was announced to the public with a press release:

> "The Italian group STET and the French group Thomson, following approval by their respective governments, have decided to move forward with the agreement to merge the semiconductor activities of SGS Microelettronica and Thomson Semiconducteurs, with each company

contributing equally. The resulting entity will be controlled 50 percent by STET and 50 percent by Thomson-CSF, with registered offices in the Netherlands. ... The new company, with the backing of the Italian and French governments, has operations in Europe, in the United States and in Asia. With revenues of nearly $800 million, [SGS Thomson] will represent an international hub ranking 14th in the world and 2nd in Europe. The new group has everything it takes to become one of the world's leading semiconductor producers."

France decided to keep two divisions out of the merger – Military and Space, and Hybrids and Microwave. For purposes of military strategy, these entities were separated from Thomson Semiconduc-teurs and remained under the conglomerate led by Gomez. But even without these two divisions, the new company was immediately rec-ognized in the international press as a global player. "The Reawaken-ing of the European Chip Industry," read the *Wall Street Journal*; the *Financial Times* depicted a venture that was betting on the "magic bil-lion" in revenues. "Italian Wedding for Thomson," was the headline in *Le Monde*, while in Italy's leading newspaper, *Corriere della Sera*, it sounded as if Europe was throwing down the gauntlet to the US and Japan: "Now we're competing on a level playing field." In Europe, the new group was bigger than Siemens, and closing in fast on Philips, Europe's top semiconductor company at the time.

Pistorio took over the leadership position, while the French kept the presidency and the operations headquarters. "The shareholders decided that I would be the CEO, probably because SGS was already in the black, so I had a proven track record for being able to turn a company around," Pistorio comments. "Jacques hadn't had the time. But in exchange, they decided the headquarters had to be Paris." So Pistorio with his wife and children set off once again, leaving Italy and moving to the French capital for ten years.

This is the origin story of SGS-Thomson Microelectronics, a ven-ture representing the final destination in a journey that began with Floriani, Olivetti, Aigrain, and the French semiconductor school. The new name was coined by Carlo E. Ottaviani, who was head of communications at the time, to reflect the experiences and histories of the two companies. Ottaviani also launched a sophisticated ad

campaign to spotlight team work, using a quote from Shakespeare's
Julius Caesar that embodied the identity of the new company:

> *"There is a tide in the affairs of men which taken at the flood leads on to fortune."*

It was the culmination of a project that had come a long way, one
deeply imprinted with an American approach, made up of intersections and connections with Shockley, Fairchild, Intel, Zilog, Texas
Instruments, Motorola, and IBM.

> "One of the reasons why things worked so well right away," recalls Alain
> Dutheil, "is that at the end of the day we weren't trying to make an
> Italian company or a French company, but an American-style company.
> We had a shared language, and a way of thinking and problem solving
> that made it clear we came from the same school, so we were in synch
> from the word go."

Silicon Europe was becoming a reality, carrying with it the legacy
of Silicon Valley, but at the same time determined to challenge the
Americans right out of the gate and carve out its own space on the
global market.

9 The European Chips that Conquered the World

The season of strategic alliances

After the merger, Pistorio got the ball rolling for the new SGS-Thomson, focusing on the five rules of its new CEO: vision, teamwork, culture, roadmap, and execution. A frenetic reorganization began between Italy and France encompassing the entire research and production apparatus of the two semiconductor leaders who had become a single player.

The hardest part came when it was time to evaluate the redundancies from the merger. SGS and Thomson were complementary in many ways, but there were inevitable duplications as well as gaps in efficiency to compensate for.

> "There were too many factories, so we had to go through a rationalization process," says Pistorio. "This meant transferring products and processes from one plant to another, and then very gradually shutting down the plants we no longer needed. That was the toughest part, the most painful process, because it meant firing people. But some plants were just hopeless cases, and we needed to invest in research and development so we could compete on a global scale and catch up with the big players."

The outcome of this process was a new map of Silicon Europe, with research and innovation concentrated at Grenoble, Rousset, Agrate, Catania, and Castelletto. Production on the continent was done in the same facilities plus Tours in France (Crolles would follow in 1993) as well as Malta, Casablanca, Carrollton in Texas (formerly Mostek),

Phoenix, and the strongholds in Asia: Singapore and Muar (Malaysia) inherited from SGS, and Penang (Malaysia) from Thomson.

In 1989, SGS-Thomson was able to announce its first profits to the market: $2 million, on revenues that hit the $1 billion mark. As the 1980s came to a close, in the global ranking of semiconductor manufacturers, the French-Italian group was positioned at number 12, and Silicon Europe's star was rising, with three main players: SGS-Thomson, Philips, and Siemens (the semiconductor branches of the latter two companies would become NXP and Infineon, respectively). They were taking control of a sizeable chunk of the market dominated by Asia and America. The top earners were NEC, Toshiba, and Hitachi from Japan, each with turnover topping $3 billion to $4 billion, followed by Motorola and Texas Instruments. Intel was jostling for position with Fujitsu, Mitsubishi, and Matsushita in the lower half of the top ten. In 1989, Philips was the European leader, at number 10 in the global rankings, but SGS-Thomson was close behind, going all-out to break into the top ten too.

The fall of the Berlin Wall, the end of the Cold War, and the opening up of Eastern European countries to the rest of the world: All this generated euphoria on the markets. But it was immediately followed by another cyclical slowdown in the semiconductor sector. The early 1990s were times of crisis triggered by excess production and surplus stock, and uncertainty in financial markets during the Gulf War.

The Italian-French company led by Pistorio was still young, but it tenaciously continued prepping the launch pad for final take-off. One of the keys to the success of SGS-Thomson model can be traced back to this moment and the choice of strategic alliances. As the embodiment of Silicon Europe, SGS-Thomson didn't want to be just another supplier to big industrials and tech groups; it wanted to partner with its customers, accompany them on their journey and work with them to realize their products: an approach that was embedded in the DNA of the Italian and French researchers and managers who led the company.

There were already vital partnerships that had been established pre-merger. In the US, for example, SGS won a key customer – Seagate – just as that American company was on the verge of becoming a world leader in the production of hard disk drives for computers. Its market capitalization was already $350 million.

The year was 1984, and it had taken some time to set up the first meeting at Seagate's headquarters in California. Finally, Bozotti and his colleague from Phoenix, Serban Coss, managed to get an appointment with the head of integrated circuits development at the American company. In Bozotti's words:

"We got to Seagate's headquarters, but the person we were supposed to talk to didn't show up for the meeting, there was no sign of him. I was furious! I had flown in from Italy for this meeting; I wanted to ditch the whole deal. But Serban convinced me to go back the next day. It was a wise move: we met the manager and convinced him to give some serious thought to BCD[1] and all its power applications. After that we met a few more times in Lugano, because he couldn't travel to Italy. He wasn't American, so there were problems getting a visa."

It was the beginning of a partnership that lasts to this day based on BCD motor controllers for hard disks.

Thomson Semiconducteurs also brought high-profile strategic partnerships to the table, such as Alcatel in telecommunications and Thomson Consumer. This last collaboration was overseen by group manager Philippe Geyres, and would lead to the creation of the US satellite television project DirecTV.

ST found another great partner in Europe, consolidating the growth of that European silicon hub, which was ready to run with the big dogs (the Americans and the Japanese). This was the client that all the big names in semiconductors dreamed of, because it was a top global supplier to practically all the major car companies, one of the industrial production areas with the strongest growth prospects for chip producers. Beyond that, it was also a thriving enterprise, solid and innovative, which in 1986 celebrated its first 100 years in business: Bosch.

In its previous French and Italian iterations, ST had made many attempts over the years to sell to the Germans in Stuttgart, but with

---

[1] We mentioned this in Chapter 1, and we'll go into more detail in Chapter 10.

little success. It was the invention of the BCD for smart power applications – added to the tenacity of Aldo Romano – that changed everything.

> "We had our fantastic new technology, but at first we couldn't even sell that to Bosch," Romano recollects. "We were very keen to win them over because they were the world's number one supplier to the auto industry. We met with them time and time again, and for years we never managed to sell them anything. They were always very interested from a technical perspective, but we could never seal the deal. Later I figured out why: they had their own internal semiconductor production and they were trying to develop the BCD themselves. Their designers felt a bit like they had to use in-house products, but they recognized the fact that we had a better technology. This is what gave us the idea to create a type of partnership which we would later replicate in other cases."

ST made Bosch a proposal: free transfer to the Germans of all ST's BCD technology plus free updates on all future process evolutions. In exchange, Bosch would give ST half of its production. As Romano says, "We told them, you produce half the BDC, we'll produce the other half, and we'll work together on design." Bosch liked the idea, and so began a strategic alliance that 30 years later is still going strong, even extending to encompass many other technologies. In any case, the Stuttgart company wasted no time in activating production of devices realized with BCD. As a result, from the 1990s on, motorists all over the world started driving cars with anti-lock brake systems (ABS), engine control systems, and even electric windows that were all controlled by BCD chips (though most people didn't know it). Half of these chips were produced in Bosch's plant in Reutlingen (in Germany) and half in ST's production facilities. The deal with Bosch became a sort of blueprint for new commercial relationships with clients all over the world, although for every partner ST had to find just the right arrangement.

In addition to the original leadership style of the team headed by Pistorio from the Paris headquarters, in these negotiations ST could bring to the table the new technologies and products that shored up ST's offering year after year. It was the end of the era when Silicon Europe only did American-licensed production and focused on the small domestic market for TVs and electric appliances. Now, French-Italian chips could go head to head with international competitors and high-quality products.

> "Custom products with proprietary technology opened the door to strategic alliances," Pistorio recollects. "But we sold all sorts of things to clients. We sold transistors, microcontrollers and CMOS; we offered basic technology and ad hoc solutions, like what happened with HP.[2] We developed a solid customer base made up of some big clients, and on that we built an organization that could withstand any crisis. ST's ten main commercial partners in the 1990s served as the company's growth engine."

In total, in 1991, these clients represented total turnover of $200 million. Ten years on, the value generated by strategic alliances had grown tenfold, to $2.2 billion.

> "One of our basic strategic guidelines," Pistorio explains, "was innovation driven by the market through strategic alliances. It was our customers who told us what products they were looking to make in the future. We offered our technologies and skills and then developed made-to-measure solutions for them. That's what we did with the Americans at HP when they came to us looking for processes linked to ink cartridges for printers. And that's what we did with the Canadians at Nortel, another one of our very first key customers. With these partners, we were able to find solutions for any kind of problem they threw at us. With HP, for instance, they asked us to take over their factory in Rancho Bernardo in California as part of our partnership agreement. Same thing with Nortel; they wanted to get rid of a factory in Ottawa."

Wall Street

Meanwhile, the market was watching that strange Italian-French company, backed by Romano Prodi's IRI and Mitterand's government, and didn't quite know what to make of the experiment that was underway.

---

[2] See Chapter 1.

Prodi considered ST a crown jewel, and Pistorio's visits always put him in a good mood.

"The president of IRI often invited CEOs of companies in the group so he could get updates from them," ST's former CEO recalls. "I would go to him, stay an hour or so, and then leave. Not long afterwards, Fabiani, who was my boss,[3] would call and ask: 'What did you tell Professor Prodi? He told me you really got him excited!' Later, when we got to know each other better, I asked him what he meant and he explained: 'Anyone who stepped into my office back then came to complain and ask for a handout. Then you would come in with your briefcase, you'd open it and start to say: "With this product, we'll hit the Americans, with this other one we'll take out the Japanese…" Then you'd close your briefcase and you'd leave. You never came crying; you came to explain what you were going to do to beat the competition.'"

But Prodi's enthusiasm was not widely shared; and skepticism prevailed with regard to ST. Pistorio sums it up like this:

"Generally speaking, lots of people thought we were crazy. Before the merger, Morgan Stanley was asked to evaluate the operation and present it to shareholders. And the conclusion was that the new-born company had would have a hard time staying afloat; the best-case scenario was it would go under to the tune of $2 billion. After the merger, Bocconi University took at stab at ST: they did an autonomous study which concluded that the company had zero chance of survival. I responded with a truism that they taught me when I was young: 'It's been scientifically proven that the albatross is too heavy to fly, but it doesn't know that, so it keeps on flying anyway.'"

The French and Italian governments did their best to help the ST albatross fly for a time, hoping it wouldn't be long before it could soar by itself. In November 1992, during the 13th French-Italian summit, French President François Mitterand and Italian Prime Minister Gi-

---

[3] Fabiano Fabiani, at the time CEO of Finmeccanica. The IRI Group company in 1989 had purchased STET's shares in the Italian-French joint venture, SGS-Thomson.

uliano Amato announced that an agreement had been reached to re-capitalize SGS-Thomson Microelectronics. The financials of the deal were later explained by the countries' industry ministers, Dominique Strauss-Kahn for France and Giuseppe Guarino for Italy. The aim of the initiative was to increase the company's capital by $1 billion over five years, starting from $500 million deposited by the end of 1992.

The capital injection came as ST was on the road to recovery after the 1990s got off to a rocky start; investments were needed to fund the ambitious growth plans of Pistorio's team. After rationalizing existing production plants, the time had come to open new, cutting-edge facilities. On September 9, 1993, with several ministers from Paris in attendance, a new production facility was inaugurated at Crolles. This was what put the Rhône-Alpes region on the map of the French microelectronics industry, and consolidated the role of Silicon Europe, which spanned both sides of Mont Blanc. Crolles became a feature of the local ecosystem that united the academic research of LETI with the production of EFCIS, and served as the stage for the debut of the production of 200mm wafers for integrated circuits with CMOS technology.

> "When Crolles opened," Joel Hartmann explains, "we no longer had much need for EFCIS, a little fab that had become obsolete and was later closed down. But more importantly, at Crolles we had set in motion another major strategic partnership with Philips Semiconductors. They were actually the competition, but at Crolles we did joint research and development and later some production too. Years after that, in 1998, again in partnership with Philips, we began contemplating the idea of a Crolles 2 specializing in 300mm wafers – a facility that opened in 2003."

In describing Crolles, this is what ST's communication department wrote at the time: "The purpose is to serve as an avant-garde center that will free Europe from dependence on the Japanese and demonstrate our ability to face any competition by realizing advanced prototype circuits."

This was the company's spirit on full display, the same spirit reflected in the challenge of breaking into the Asian market as well as the American market. The approach Pistorio wanted to take was an integrated one.

"In Asia we had to have marketing, a design center, assembly and distribution," Pistorio explains. "The same was true for America. But seeing how in the US, back in the day of SGS, we had nothing, we decided to start from scratch and take a greenfield approach. In other words, to build our own factory. When we had to choose the site, I picked Phoenix because I knew the area well, and Motorola was located there too. First, we opened a marketing department, then a design center and finally the factory. The Americans, like many Europeans, were skeptical. They thought our governments would quickly get fed up and we wouldn't get very far."

Instead, ST kept watching its revenues mushroom; it was going great guns. Landing in the US was not only a manufacturing move; it was a financial one too. To convince the world to take ST seriously, the company had to appear on the most prominent investor stage: Wall Street. "One day," Pistorio recounts, "I decided that SGS-Thomson was ready to go public. I began to discuss it with the shareholders and, as usual, I found them reluctant – especially the Italians. But we went ahead anyway."

As the day dawned on December 8, 1994, in a freezing cold Manhattan, Pistorio, Dutheil, and a small group of ST colleagues met in the lobby of a large New York City hotel. Two black limos were waiting outside to take them quickly to Wall Street, where at 8:00 am they were being hosted for breakfast by the top management of the New York Stock Exchange. In the Exchange's oval ceremony room, Jean-Pierre Noblanc (president of ST's Supervisory Board) along with the chiefs of the world's leading financial institution were waiting for Pistorio and his group. After coffee, they moved to the trading floor, which was crowded with traders in their colored coats, wearing special shoes that wouldn't ruin the hardwood floors. At 9:30 sharp, the opening bell rang and on the digital ticker tape running along the walls of the trading floor displaying share prices, a message flashed by: "Welcome, SGS-Thomson!"

Silicon Europe had disappointed the expectations of the skeptics who considered it a lost cause from the start. ST was now listed on the New York Stock Exchange, and made its debut on the Paris stock exchange on the same day. In New York, it traded at 22.50 dollars per share; in Paris at 119.5 francs per share, for a total market cap in excess of 2 billion dollars after the first day of trading.

Cellphone fever

Bosch was the first major partnership that formed the foundations for the future ST, but an even greater alliance came from Finland: a partner that became a crucial growth driver for the Italian-French company, and continued to be so for over ten years, but ultimately turned into a serious criticality. Like every company in the mobile phone industry during the two decades spanning the new millennium, ST rode the roller-coaster rise and spectacular fall of the one-time colossus: Nokia.

The story of this Finnish multinational has been the subject of case studies in management courses the world over for years. It once played a leading role in the market of cellphones and later smartphones, but the Nokia brand is usually associated with other firms such as Kodak and Blockbuster that were allegedly guilty of "being incapable of understanding innovation." Of course, the story is a bit more complicated than that. But there is no doubt that from 2005 to 2010, many of the regrettable choices made at Nokia sadly canceled out all the success of the decade prior.

Nokia was founded in 1865 in the Finnish town of the same name. In the beginning, it outperformed all its competitors in the telephony industry. For instance, the first completely portable cellphone was a Nokia product, launched in 1987. The GSM standard, which set off the explosion in mobile telephony, had been developed mainly by the Scandinavian company, together with Siemens. And it's no co-incidence that the first phone call in the world over a GSM network was made from a government office in Finland on July 1, 1991. The following year, the Nokia 1011 became the first GSM mobile phone on the market.

In 1998, the company became the biggest cellphone seller in the world, with $20 billion in revenues and $2.6 billion in profits. Not long after, the Nokia 1100 smashed all cellphone sales records.[4] At its peak in 2000 (the year of the New Economy and dot-com fever), Nokia counted 55,000 employees and on its own represented 4 per-

---

[4] Production of the Nokia 1100 stopped in 2009, but it is still the best-selling cellphone in the world: over 250 million sold in 190 countries.

cent of Finland's GDP and 21 percent of the country's exports. Its share of the global cellphone market at that time was 30 percent, nearly double that of Motorola, its closest rival.

Nokia looked unstoppable, and that's when the company set up a strategic partnership with ST that would be a springboard for growth in both companies. "When we worked with Nokia, that was a great time, and it overlapped a bit ST's golden age, when we really took off after we went public," Bozotti recounts. The partnership was finalized in March 1994, while Nokia was riding the tidal wave of demand for GSM cellphones. The company had already conquered 20 percent of the global mobile phone market, even defying the Japanese on their home turf. Here too, as with Bosch, the alliance had the feel of a rebirth for Silicon Europe, bringing together a slate of technological competencies to take on American and Asian multinationals.

Thanks to an innovative design methodology invented in Grenoble, ST guaranteed Nokia rapid development and production times for the microelectronic components in analog CMOS technology for power management applications and RF. These required constant updates to keep up with lightning-fast expansion in mobile telephony. The world was discovering internet and mobile phones, and demand for chips was skyrocketing. The alliance held strong for fifteen years or so, only to later collapse when Nokia began to make missteps in the mobile phone market. But in the 1990s, the collaboration with Nokia helped consolidate the inner core of partners that also included Alcatel, Thomson Consumer, Bosch, Nortel, Seagate, and HP, with more new members on the way.

The century closed with an ST that seemed to have travelled light-years since the critical years of SGS-ATES and Thomson Semiconducteurs. The company was standing firmly on its own two feet, and in 1998 broke into the ranking of the world's top ten semiconductor producers. With Philips in eighth place, ST in ninth, and Siemens in tenth, Silicon Europe had become a global powerhouse. For Pistorio and his team, it was time for the company to move forward without carrying the weight of its old shareholders. And so Thomson sold its shares in 1998 and the company changed its name, for the last time, to STMicroelectronics. At the same time, the controlling Italian shareholders (IRI and Comitato SIR) and their French counterparts

(France Telecom and CEA Industrie) started pulling out, freeing up a large chunk of shares and allowing ST to be listed on the Milan Stock Exchange.

The company formerly run by Floriani, Olivetti, and Fairchild, which had merged with the heirs to the French semiconductor industry, debuted on the Borsa in Milan among the top ten equities listed on the Italian stock exchange, and in fifth place among nonfinancial equities, behind ENI, TIM, Telecom, and FIAT.[5]

The 2000s dawned with very optimistic prospects. Although Pistorio continued his work with passion, he was reaching the end of another three-year term as CEO of ST, and in theory it was almost time for him to retire. But only in theory, not quite yet. There were still many other challenges to face. Before finding out what they were, it's worthwhile to go back to the beginning of our journey and stop off in the research labs and production hubs in Silicon Europe to get a clearer understanding of some of the crucial areas of technological innovation underpinning ST's success, beginning in the 1980s. Once again, these are stories of innovation, creativity, intuition, and a European approach to global technology.

---

[5] "*ST in Borsa, sarà tra le top ten*" [ST on the Stock Exchange will be in the Top Ten], *Corriere della Sera* (Milan), June 4, 1998, p. 27.

10   The Winning Hand of Innovation

Model airplanes and chips

The SGS-Thomson merger formed the foundations for fully exploiting analog skills and experience with amplification in Italy, and the expertise in image management and digital telephony in France. This marked the start of a relaunch that would give SGS-Thomson (later STMicroelectronics) the impetus to regain ground on all fronts. Ultimately, Silicon Europe's chips would be running inkjet printer processes and electronic meters, packing video game consoles and smartphones with billions of components, and controlling the most delicate processes in the automobile sector, as well as automation in factories and in the future-forward space industry. Beginning in the 1980s, this evolution would further advance technologies developed in previous decades, and continue to the present day with the Internet of Things (IoT), artificial intelligence, self-driving cars, and infotainment.

Even when Italy and France were going through difficult times, even when it seemed as if the semiconductor industry was to be short lived, innovations were emerging. And these innovations provided a base to build on. The first European integrated circuits had already appeared – developed entirely in-house – the first ever to target the mass market. Also made in Silicon Europe were the first such circuits for both the automotive industry and for telecommunications.

But above all else, what made their mark were certain technologies that formed a winning hand and still enjoy success today. Hiding behind their puzzling acronyms are incredible stories. To understand the success of Silicon Europe, we have to explore BCD, MEMS, image sensors, and FD-SOI – silicon technologies that represent four decades of European innovation. Lots of capital letters and complicated names (because in the field of semiconductors we always use acronyms). But by telling the story of what these abbreviations stand for and how they came to be, their meaning will no longer be the exclusive domain of industry insiders. And that's the way it should be, because in actual fact our lives are filled with these devices. They're everywhere, and whether we know it or not, we use them every single day.

Let's start with BCD technology. The perfect place to begin this story is at the entrance of the STMicroelectronics plant in Agrate Brianza. Because here, since 2021, the first thing visitors see is one of the prestigious "milestones" awarded by the Institute of Electrical and Electronics Engineers (IEEE), the most important organization in the world for the promotion of technological sciences, with global headquarters in Piscataway, New Jersey. An IEEE milestone (which is actually a large plaque with a golden frame) is like a Nobel prize of technology, honoring inventions and discoveries that have truly changed the history of the field. In the entire world, fewer than 200 have ever been awarded, and one of them is hanging at the Agrate entrance in recognition of the invention of BCD.

Before explaining what this is all about, we need to get a bit better acquainted with a person whom we've already met many times before. He fathered BCD while heading a team of young talents. "If there is a Lost Tribe of Silicon Valley, it resides here on a broad industrial plain on the outskirts of Milan, and the tribe's leader is 62-year-old Bruno Murari," read a full-page article in the *New York Times* in the late 1990s. It went on to describe what it called a "Renaissance craftsmen's guild" of silicon, created by the descendants of *Fairchild*.[1]

There is something in every inventor's childhood that gives them a special lens, allowing them to see things differently than others do.

---

[1] John Markoff, "In Milan, a Subtle Artisan Finds a Medium in New Analog Chips," *New York Times*, July 27, 1998.

The place where they grew up, what their home life was like, the hobbies they took up, and passions they developed when they were young – all these are the seeds of creativity that will bear fruit when they become adults. For example, Bob Noyce, one of the fathers of the microchip, was the third of four children of a Congregationalist pastor, an anti-establishment "island" in the protestant archipelago. Raised in a small town of rural Iowa, he spent a lot of time in the lab that his father had built in the basement of their home, building thermionic-valve radios, propeller-powered sleds, and even a hang-glider. "I grew up in the American countryside," Noyce recounted. "You had to do stuff on your own: if something broke, you had to fix it yourself."[2]

But of all the singular childhoods of all the inventors in our story, the most unique has to be Bruno Murari's. As a child he had an entire island to explore. He was born in 1936 in his mother's hometown of Treviso, and when he was only 40 days old, his family moved to the island of San Giorgio in the lagoon of Venice, where he would live for the first 15 years of his life. His father was a military man, chief marshal of mountain artillery, assigned to the arms and munitions depot on the island. On San Giorgio there were three or four officers, seven noncommissioned officers, some 30 soldiers and their families. It was a small world where every morning, the island's inhabitants would wake to the stunning sight of Saint Mark's Square and the Doge Palace. Bruno would go to school every day by boat, listening for the sounds of the church bells so he wouldn't get lost when it was foggy. "We were a group of wild kids with an entire island at our disposal, where we could play cowboys and Indians, and countless soccer games," Murari recalls.

Young Bruno learned the art of do-it-yourself, and he channeled it into his special passion: model airplanes. "I got back to San Giorgio after a vacation in Trentino with a box of broken wings and spare parts given to me by a kid who made model airplanes," Murari remembers. "I began to study by myself, then when I was ten, I started taking a weekly model airplane course." Studying the secrets of

---

[2] Robert Noyce, interviewed in the documentary "Silicon Valley," *American Experience*, PBS, 2013.

flight, building materials, and radio controls opened the floodgates of creativity for Murari. "First, I worked with a razor blade, balsa wood, a little bit of poplar wood. The idea was to start with research, from an idea written down on paper, and then develop that intuition into a project. Building the first prototypes, testing them, seeing if they worked, trouble shooting, trying to fix mistakes and starting over." It was an approach that eventually made Murari a model airplane champion.

Faggin also shares this passion with his colleague: "But Bruno is much better than I am," the Silicon Valley entrepreneur admits. Over the years, Murari participated in hundreds of model airplane competitions; he was crowned champion of Italy six times and world champion once. To this day he continues to follow his passion, even though he is well into his 80s. The method he learned when he was building flying machines coupled with a creative island childhood are the ingredients that undeniably contributed to the lateral thinking Murari used when he and his team tackled various projects in the field of semiconductors. And the most exemplary case, without a doubt, is BCD.

The acronym BCD is a synthesis of process technology that combines – in a single chip – high-precision analog bipolar transistors (B) with CMOS logic transistors with high-performance digital switching systems (C), and high-powered DMOS transistors (D). In simpler terms, what happened in the mid-1980s was this: the researchers at Agrate and Castelletto managed to take the best of bipolar technology from the 1950s, and add the groundbreaking CMOS logic that led to the digital boom of the 1960s. (Note that still today CMOS controls the most complex digital circuits. A modern smartphone is embedded with microchips containing 6-7 billion CMOS transistors.) The final ingredient was robust, high-tension DMOS power components developed in the 1970s. And all this on a single silicon semiconductor die.

The result is smartpower technology that has enabled chip designers to combine analog and digital power signal processing in a flexible, reliable way. Since the BCD process went into production in 1985, ST has sold over 40 billion devices built from 5 million silicon wafers. And the technology behind it all, now in its tenth generation, is used all over: in the automotive industry, in industrial process automation and robotics, in all engine control technologies in general and in smartphones, household appliances, speakers, hard disks in computers, power units, printers, medical equipment, and modems. We may not even know it, but BCD technologies are by our side every day. They've made it possible for small signals and big power to cohabitate a single chip, overcoming challenges such as overheating, dispersion, and various other chemical and physical reactions.

"Before BCD," says Bozotti, "our researchers had already developed smartpower audio circuits on a single chip, and this was the seminal experience they were building on. An audio circuit is a product that has a controller: a low-level electric signal is magnified and then goes into a power amplifier that controls the speaker. Our researchers already realized that these products had a very high level of dissipation, because there was still no way to have integrated digital control. This problem lay in the internal architecture, and the laws of physics and electronics. The brainwave they had was to substitute this type of product, where they had already combined the power stages with some form of analog control, with more advanced solutions. This meant integrating a CMOS digital control too, and replacing the bipolar power with more robust and efficient DMOS devices. We immediately used the same approach for applications other than audio, and the first BCD product we rolled out in 1985 was a driver for engines coupled with interface logic for microprocessors."

Murari headed up the process from the research center in Castelletto, joining the skills of his team in bipolar technology with the work of a few talented young researchers at Agrate on CMOS and DMOS. What ultimately led them to BCD was continuously sharing ideas and running practical experiments that Murari encouraged everyone to do using the pragmatic method he had developed during his early years on the island of San Giorgio.

"We can't say that there's a single person who invented the BCD," explains Aldo Romano, who led the business unit Murari and his team worked in at the time. "Actually, it came out of conversations over a cup of coffee. That's why I am fairly skeptical about the idea that in the future, all work will be based on smart working. We made these technological advances thanks in part to the personal relationships that had formed; you can't put a price on that. Many other labs were trying to do what we did with BCD, but they failed to strike the right balance between the technologies, and I think that the difference for us was our work method."

As BCD was an exclusive ST technology, it was also an opportunity to open new markets and scout for new customers, especially in the US, where SGS and Thomson had never been able to gain a foothold. "We managed to carve out our own market niche and maintain a leadership position," Romano affirms. "With BCD, for the first time we got a foot in the door of new clients and once that door was open with one product, everything was easier: selling the second product takes one-tenth the initial effort. BCD was our battering ram."

Alain Dutheil agrees:

"BCD technology is what really opened up the American market for us. It was a field where Texas Instruments and Motorola had nothing to offer. Instead, we jumped in, and not just for printers, but for computer hard disks too. A while back, I opened up a hard disk drive on a computer and it was full of ST products, which had started being used in computers around that time."

But BCDs are not part of past for semiconductors. Far from it. "This technology will be extremely useful in the future as well," explains Joel Hartmann, for many years the head of CMOS research and development for STMicroelectronics.

"We're not the only ones who produce them; today there are a number of companies that copied what we were promoting years ago, because this technology is a gold mine with dozens of applications. So currently there's competition, and that's always a good thing because it pushes us to innovate, to try to shrink the size of the circuit design even more to make the power we offer even 'smarter.' At first, the dimensions we were working on were one micron, then 0.8 microns, then we went ever smaller. Now we're developing 40-nanometer BCD technology, which soon will be destined for the production of 300mm wafers in the new fab in Agrate."

Measuring speed

"Innovation is linked to the desire to do something better than the competition," comments Murari. "The race, the competition, they help: if you want to finish at the top, you have to work better than everyone else and find solutions that you can actually realize. You always have to study the whole process, up to actually making the product, from conception to complete industrialization. What you need is that manual dexterity you develop as a kid. In fact, it was the kids we used to call 'nerds' who had it (or model airplane builders like myself); today we call them 'makers.' Ideas also come up when you have the habit of thinking in a certain way."

After the invention of BCD, ST applied the same approach for another category of technological "jewels": Micro-Electro-Mechanical Systems (MEMS). With this product category, we move from one field of action to another – from smart power to smart things. This a world teeming with compact, precise, and economical silicon sensors and actuators. And it's these minuscule sensors that measure movement such as linear and angular acceleration, as well as pressure, temperature, and humidity.

MEMS were not invented by STMicroelectronics. The study of how to make MOS transistors interact with the analog world – including movements – had already begun in the 1960s in the US and was progressing in different corners of the globe. The term MEMS appeared in the 1980s and many companies and academic research institutions investigated these systems. But Romano, Murari, and their team focused on a very specific field and managed to put many ideas into practice that very often had previously only been theories.

Romano recollects: "The brilliant idea was to focus on devices that were essentially accelerometers and gyroscopes that could move on three axes. In other words, these were objects that could take information on their movement and transform it into a digital signal." It was the beginning of a long road, one that allows our phones to tell us how many steps we've taken during the day, and enables our game console to create the illusion of playing tennis in the living room, and makes our airbags inflate if an accident happens (and only then). All of these are activities controlled by MEMS technology sensors.

"Our adventure with MEMS started in 1992," says Murari, "at a European Solid-State Circuits and Devices (ESSCIRC) conference, where I was chairman. Professor Henry Baltez, from the University of Zurich, came and told us that he had used silicon to create pressure transducers. Then he showed us some pictures and I fell in love with this thing because it showed that mechanics is analog, just like the human brain to some extent. Digital is numbers and it's hard for me to translate them into projects; for that you need more intelligent people than myself, like Faggin."

Murari continues,

"I started to study on my own, to look into what could be done on a chip in terms of measuring pressure, acceleration and other phenomena. We began to run some tests, using mechanical parts and CMOS. A few years later, a professor from the University of Berkeley came to visit us in Castelletto. He told us about the research they were doing in this field, and I realized that if we wanted to make the leap with our silicon technologies in terms of quality, we had to send one of our engineers to study at Berkeley and bring us back the knowhow we needed."

A young man hired less than a month earlier was tapped for the job; he would end up heading the MEMS unit, and one of ST's product groups as well. His name was Benedetto Vigna.

"He spent a year and a half at Berkeley," says Murari. "We spoke every week and he would update us and give us information that allowed us to move forward with the MEMS project. In time, Benedetto learned who the best people in the field were, and who had the best production and the best machines. Having him in California gave us a competitive edge. In the meantime, here we were trying to solve the problems that came up while we were exploring accelerometers. We used two chips, separating the mechanical part and the digital part, and then assembled them a single package that looked like one single chip. But there were problems, mostly related to the pressure generated by the polymerization of the package resin, which deformed the silicon substrate as the room temperature varied. This resulted in poorer performance."

Murari continues,

"The solution came to me in an unusual way. I went to Japan for work and while I was in a room showing our products to four or five other engineers, there was an earthquake. My immediate reaction, obviously, was to get to a safe place, maybe under a table, but the others very calmly explained to me that we were in an earthquake-proof building. We ended up talking about Japanese buildings, and how they had dealt with the problem of earthquakes in the past. The engineers explained to me that the solution came from observing nature. When an earthquake strikes, they told me, forests don't collapse and the trees remain standing; they are flexible. The pagoda was a building inspired by forests, with various levels and a single 'tree' as a base. When the floor moves, due to jolting tremors or wave-like motion from an earthquake, the floors have some degree of inertia, but the flexible tree absorbs and cushions the movement. On my flight home, as I was thinking this over, it occurred to me to try and use the same approach for MEMS."

From this insight came a new process that involved suspending the two parts of the accelerometer – the stator and the rotor – by using an architecture similar to a pagoda, which prevents friction and guarantees flexibility. This approach enabled ST to upgrade the quality of its products in one fell swoop. "When Vigna came back," continues Murari, "together we starting building what was probably the first triple-axis accelerometer in the world." That was the innovation the *New York Times* was talking about in 1998 when it dedicated a full page to Murari, and this new device was ready in just a few years. But it didn't debut in a car, or an electronic appliance, or a mobile phone. Instead, it made its first appearance in a videogame console: Nintendo's Wii. With this revolutionary gaming system, users hold controllers that detect movement and enable never-before-seen experiences. It was one of the most successful home entertainment devices ever invented, with more than 100 million units sold. And it was made possible by Murari's "pagoda" MEMS.

"The difference between designing analog and digital electronic devices has long been viewed by many engineers as the difference between an art and a science," wrote the *New York Times* in the story on Castelletto. In the article, Richard Chesson, a Canadian engineer who worked under Murari in the Castelletto lab, is quoted as saying: "Digital design is like building with Lego blocks. Analog design is more like wood carving to get sculptures."[3]

---

[3] Markoff, "Subtle Artisan Finds a Medium."

Interest in this unusual technology began to proliferate among customers, and it wasn't just Nintendo with the Wii. Others were lining up too, including Toshiba, which built an innovative product using ST's device. It was a drop-proof laptop, which many of us will remember from the advertisements that came out for it at the time. This product owed its success to ST's accelerometers, which could "sense" if the computer was falling, and then lock damage-protection systems into place to shield the read/write head and the surface of the hard drive. Another application was developed for washing machines. ST's devices detected the level of vibrations the machine was subjected to and regulated the spin cycle to start only after optimal draining to eliminate excess water from the laundry; this reduced the machine's movement in the room. Then came handheld computers, evolved cellphones, and smartphones, where MEMS could signal whether the user was holding the device horizontally or vertically; they could also measure steps and movements. Today MEMS can monitor bodily functions, from breathing to heart rate, and we find other important applications in the automotive sector, where accelerometers and gyroscopes are everywhere. They are critical components in self-driving cars too.

Time of Flight

The focus of the wood carvers at ST (to use the *New York Times*'s description) was not limited to analog with BCD and MEMS; quite the contrary. On the French side of the Alps in particular, they were successfully cultivating and exploiting their experience working in silicon using purely digital technologies, like optical sensors that measure Time of Flight. In other words, these sensors can calculate distance by emitting photons and measuring the time it takes for them to return. The Grenoble district had been on a long journey in the field of imaging, often blazing the trail. Since the days of Thomson, semiconductor applications for imaging were being studied, and LETI's deep academic research always allowed Silicon Europe to keep abreast of international innovations on this front.

The complex sphere of image management has always been the

focus of the French electronics school, which over the years has succeeded in moving images away from traditional supports (television,
cameras) and taking them into the world of digital pixels. Initially computers and later smartphones began recording and conveying
visual experiences; they gradually came to dominate the video and
photography industries. In this transition, the French contingent in
Silicon Europe played a key role in supplying the necessary technology, especially optical sensors.

One of ST's ideas that paid off in this field was to search out
the best innovations on the market and then combine them with
in-house research. In the field of imaging sensors, for example, researchers at the University of Edinburgh made some notable progress in the latter half of the 1980s. They had been studying the
earliest CMOS sensors, and in 1986 they began to present the first
groundbreaking papers to the scientific community. In 1990, inspired by this research, an innovative startup called VLSI Vision
was founded in the university, which opened the door to new possi-
bilities in terms of digitalizing images. ST acquired VLSI Vision in
1999, incorporated its camera process activities, and established its
first Imaging Division.

First at Rousset and later at Crolles, ST began producing CMOS
sensors for digital image management that merged the research of
Edinburgh with the skills acquired at Grenoble. The aim was to respond to market demand, which initially centered on the first digital
cameras, but soon expanded to include cellphones. Thanks to this
move, when the Japanese began to experiment with putting digital
cameras on phones, the French were quick to respond. In 1999, at the
Japan Electronics Show, Kyocera presented the first mobile phone
with a built-in Sharp camera, and the Japanese telephone company
NTT DoCoMo brought the first models of the camera phone to the
market. Sharp, for its part, launched its own camera phone in 2000,
followed quickly by the Koreans at Samsung.

ST immediately responded to this new challenge by making a
camera for Nokia. "At first when Nokia started asking us for this
kind of thing, we wondered: 'Why ever would anyone want to put
a camera in a phone?'" recalls Eric Aussedat, who joined ST as an
engineer in 1981 and over the years became the point person for the

group's research and production on imaging.[4] "They were obviously right; they could foresee what was happening to mobile telephony and they moved really fast. And so did we." The two companies set a new industry standard, Standard Mobile Imaging Architecture (SMIA), and in 2001, ST's Bouskoura plant near Casablanca became the birthplace for the first prototype of a camera for cellphones, dubbed Matisse. The following year it went into production for Nokia.

That moment marked the start of a race to add more and more pixels on a camera; in other words, to upgrade the image resolution of the photos that a cellphone could take. ST developed various models with Nokia, and the market expanded suddenly in 2003 with the launch of the first front-facing cameras, which today we use mainly for selfies (and for face recognition). The first mobile phones to be equipped with this kind of camera were produced by NEC, Motorola, and Sony Ericsson.

Crolles kept coming out with new CMOS sensors that could handle image capture processes in more and more sophisticated ways, with an eye to enhancing resolution and eventually placing mobile phones on a par with digital cameras. In this field, the mark of distinction – and the true signature move of Silicon Europe – was the work on Time of Flight, a principle based on the speed of light. The patented FlightSense technology, which made ST one of the global leaders in the sector, consists of an emitter that sends photons towards a target and a receiver that recaptures the photons when they return. With these sensors, measuring the round-trip time of flight based on the speed of light, is an extremely accurate calculation. This can be used to determine the distance of an object when it's in the frame of a smartphone camera, for example. The applications are myriad, from focusing the camera correctly to calculating the distance between the phone and the user's ear.

Flightsense represents a highly sophisticated and constantly evolving sphere of technology that is opening the door to applications in other fields too, such as robotics, artificial intelligence, and drones

---

[4] Former Executive Vice President and General Manager of ST's Imaging Division. He retired in 2023.

(e.g. obstacle detection). Its successful track record over time has proven to be among the longest for an ST product, an ace in the company's winning hand of technologies. And thanks to FlightSense, Silicon Europe has won the trust of important Silicon Valley partners, as we shall see.

Silicon cladding

As always, the semiconductor industry is on a continual quest to comply with Moore's Law, striving to meet the constant demands of the IT industry for bigger computing power packed into smaller spaces. Shrinking chips and boosting power, year after year, is no mean feat; eventually, this quest came up against laws of physics, and problems began to emerge. It's an extremely complicated thing to control the electrical behavior of transistors that are so small they are measured in nanometers.

It is in this complex context that another proprietary ST technology plays a vital role: FD-SOI (which we'll explain below). Here's Hartmann:

"The challenge we were responding to with FD-SOI goes back to the lab work we were doing at LETI, where we first developed this technology. We had CMOS transistors that were working really well; they were critical factors that led to the computer boom. But making transistors that were getting smaller and smaller meant it was harder and harder to control dispersion. Ideally, what everybody wants is for a transistor behave like a light switch: applying voltage to a transistor is like turning on a light; cutting off that voltage it is like turning off the switch so that no current passes through it. Thirty years ago, this was fairly simple to do, because transistors were still relatively large. When we reached the nanometric scale, that's where the problems started, because when you're working on deep layers of silicon in such small devices, it's extremely difficult to create a real insulator that prevents dispersion. So it's complicated to make the transistor work like an on-off switch: there is always a little bit of leakage that compromises proper functioning."

The solution they developed at LETI, which was later transferred to the ST production facility at Crolles, was to insert an ultra-thin but effective insulating layer between the various layers of silicon. If, as we suggested in Chapter 2, creating a semiconductor in silicon is like constructing a building (with its floors, stairs, elevators, and concrete pillars), the purpose of FD-SOI is to act like cladding, which insulates the entire building. But we're talking about cladding that is less than 100 nanometers thick.

FD-SOI stands for Fully Depleted Silicon-On-Insulator. To explain, by creating an ultra-thin silicon substrate supported on an insulator, that is, Silicon-On-Insulator, it is possible to develop a fully depleted transistor architecture, very efficient from an energy consumption point of view.

Why does it matter? Because it offers the answer for overcoming countless challenges in the development of latest-generation devices for the automotive sector; it paves the way for a plethora of innovations pertaining to the IoT; and it is vital to research in the most future-forward field there is – space – also because it is more resistant to cosmic radiation than traditional CMOS circuits. "To understand why we need this energy efficiency in microscopic contexts," Hartmann explains, "all you have to do is think about what it means to have sensors that can do their jobs without wasting energy; that means the microscopic batteries that power them that can last for ten or twenty years with no recharging. In the 'on' position, these devices require very little energy, and when switched to the 'off' position, they consume next to nothing."

It doesn't take much imagination to realize that these are exactly what we humans will need the day we attempt to embark on a journey that will last years: the voyage to Mars. For the time being, and with this voyage on the horizon, FD-SOI devices produced at the Crolles facility are getting lots of practice on satellites in orbit and running several digital processes.

The challenge for the future of this type of technology is also contingent on R&D costs, which rise as devices shrink in size. But this constant pursuit of Moore's Law at some point can become unprofitable for companies such as ST. At Crolles, they're currently working on 14-nanometer technologies, but in the world of microprocessors, demand is growing for even smaller sizes: 7, 5, even 3 nanometers. These are competitive arenas where few companies dare to venture:

TSMC from Taiwan, South Korea's Samsung, Intel in the US. The issue here is not only technological, but economical as well. So Silicon Europe, in light of its origin story and track record, opted out of this market.

> "The development of these technologies is exponential in terms of R&D costs, investments and design, and even the number of wafers that you have to manufacture before you reach the right yield," Hartmann explains. "Here's an example: 20 years ago, when we developed 18 nanometer technology, we went through about a thousand wafers, at our expense. In other words, before we could sell products and send them to our clients, we had to test them on about a thousand wafers to attain an efficient level of yield. So that process was economically sustainable with a thousand slices of silicon.
>
> "When we transitioned to 14 nanometers – seeing as they were more complex, with more layers, more levels of metal, and smaller dimensions – a thousand wafers weren't enough; it took 10,000. If you move into other dimensions, the 10,000 testing wafers become 50,000. For 7- and 5-nanometer technologies, you're somewhere in the range of 100,000 wafers that you need to use internally before you can go to the client. To absorb these initial costs, there has to be a market that guarantees a return on investment worth billions of dollars. That's why we chose to stop at a certain point, because going beyond that was no longer worth it. With the exception of Intel, only TSMC and Samsung make these things because they're silicon foundries; that's why they're the suppliers to almost all semiconductor manufacturers."

BCD, MEMS, FD-SOI, light sensors, and microcontrollers: the history and evolution of all these technologies are interwoven with the last 40 years of activity and innovation in Silicon Europe. And since the 1980s, the French-Italian chip industry has bulked up its product catalog and made up for the delays that had accumulated in previous decades. Now, it was taking center stage for the next scene: the digital revolution of the 21st century.

11   Growing While Storms Are Raging

The dot-com bubble

After more than twenty years, it is still hard to fully understand what caused the digital frenzy that swept across the globe at the turn of the century, with particular intensity in the US. What would go down in history as the "dot-com bubble" was the result of the convergence of several different phenomena that caused the Nasdaq Composite Stock Market Index[1] to peak at 5,048 points on March 10, 2000. In five short years, from 1995 to 2000, the Nasdaq gained 400 percent, driven by a run on the market for tech shares, for the most part issued by newly created companies.

By the end of the 1990s, the Internet and mobile telephony were exploding, computer hardware and software sales were booming, and a new generation of aggressive venture capitalists was coming of age. All these phenomena created the conditions for the rise of digital companies of every shape and size, all with website domain names ending in ".com." Low interest rates were available to all, and everybody wanted to invest in companies that promised meteoric growth and easy money. In 1999 alone, as many as 12 companies listed on the Nasdaq started the year with their share prices at a minimum of $5, to

---

[1] NASDAQ, headquartered in New York, is a stock exchange specializing in the technology industry. In the world ranking terms of capitalization, it is second only to the New York Stock Exchange.

then see that number skyrocket by over 1,000 percent. And it wasn't just startups. For example, Qualcomm, an ST competitor with a deep specialization in digital, saw its share value soar by an eye-popping 2,619 percent in one year.[2]

Superbowl 2000 was the thermometer for measuring dot-com fever. Every year, the pro football final is the most-watched television program in the US, so advertising slots are highly coveted and come with high price tags. For the 2000 game, of 61 brands that bought precious air time for their TV ads (paying up to $2 million for 30 seconds), one-third were dot-coms, and many of them newly created.

Obviously, it couldn't last forever. And it didn't.

On April 14, 2000, the first downturn came, with NASDAQ losing 9 percent in a single day of trading. That was the moment the bubble burst and a downward spiral began, which didn't stop until 2002. Many promising companies went up in smoke and many ambitious investors went bankrupt. Accelerating the crash were the terrorist attacks on US soil on September 11, 2001. And further impetus came from two massive financial scandals that left Enron and WorldCom in ruins. In October 2002, when the avalanche came to a halt, NASDAQ had cratered to 1,114.11 points, a loss of 78 percent compared to its 2000 peak.[3] Five trillion dollars of market capitalization wiped out in the span of two years.[4]

The semiconductor industry, because of the strong ties it has always had to the computer and telecommunications sectors, could not escape unscathed from such a scenario. And the companies most invested in digital technology (such as Qualcomm and Intel) weren't the only ones that ended up in a weaker position. ST and its peers with more diversified product portfolios suffered too. Indeed, the ripple effect was felt through the entire chip industry.

---

[2] Floyd Norris, "The Year in the Markets; 1999: Extraordinary Winners and More Losers," *New York Times,* January 3, 2000, p. 17.

[3] Chris Alden, "Looking Back on the Crash," *Guardian* (London), March 10, 2005.

[4] Chris Gaither and Dawn C. Chmielewski, "Fears of Dot-Com Crash, Version 2.0," *Los Angeles Times,* July 16, 2006.

"2001 was the worst year ever in the history of semiconductors," recalls Pistorio. "Semiconductors are cyclical, they have three or four years of expansion and then crisis strikes, triggered by surplus production, a price collapse or something else. But never before had there been a time like 2001. The market collapsed; profits collapsed. ST barely managed to stay in the black, but we felt the effects of the situation all the same. I was supposed to retire that year because I was turning 65, and that was the rule. At ST the CEO gets nominated for a three-year term by the board, and another mandate for me was not part of the plan. But seeing the global situation, the president of our Supervisory Board, Jean-Pierre Noblanc, asked me to stay on. 'Pasquale,' he told me, 'You can't go and leave everything in the hands of your successor in a time of crisis and turmoil like this.' So I agreed to stay for another three years."

ST felt the effects of the crisis, but the Italian-French company was solid at this point, and strong enough to withstand market fluctuations. In 1999 revenues topped $5 billion, with sales equally divided between Europe and Asia (about 33 percent each) and a strong presence in the US (accounting for 24 percent of turnover). At the beginning of the millennium, the Group's 38,000 employees were spread across 18 manufacturing sites and 12 research hubs – and all these facilities were being continuously renovated. In May 2000, for example, Pistorio welcomed French Prime Minister Lionel Jospin and Minister of Justice Elisabeth Guigou to Rousset, in Provence. Since the days of Eurotechnique, this was a hub of the French semiconductor industry, second in importance only to Grenoble. The reason for the visit was the grand opening of the brand-new factory for producing 200mm wafers, destined to become one of the crown jewels of Silicon Europe and a growth driver. To demonstrate the potential of the semiconductors manufactured in-house, on display was a fully loaded Fiat Multipla (a compact MPV) featuring innovative digital infotainment, which Jospin had fun playing with.[5]

The company had become the protagonist not only of Silicon Europe, but also a top global player as well. After the long ascent that

---

[5] Stefano Cingolani, "Sul banco 4mila miliardi" ["Four Billion on the Table"], *Corriere della Sera* (Milan), May 22, 2000.

began with the merger of SGS and Thomson, the new ST had almost attained the same heights as the global semiconductor leaders. Even Motorola, Pistorio's former home, was now lagging far behind, in part because of the dot-com crisis. This turmoil brought hard times for the company owned by the Galvin family, which was already struggling to keep up with Nokia in mobile telephony. In 2002, the year the NASDAQ downslide stopped, with $6.4 billion in revenues ST was a hair short of Texas Instruments ($6.7 billion), but well ahead of Motorola in the field of semiconductors ($4.8 billion).[6] And then somebody started spreading the rumor that the French-Italian Silicon Europe might be ready to bite a piece out of the land of chips: America. After all, this country had produced some of ST's top managers.

ST's growth had been organic, for the most part. In other words, it came from an increase in market share, not from acquisitions or mergers with other companies in the sector. There was one exception in 2002, the acquisition of the electronics activities of French company Alcatel. But it was a relatively small transaction ($378 million) that didn't change the size of the new European semiconductor leader.

But Motorola was something else entirely.

On the morning of October 15, 2002, a story appeared on the front page of the *Financial Times*. Citing high level sources in the French government, it claimed that Pistorio was trying to make "the dream of his life" come true by acquiring Motorola.[7] According to the financial daily, the Italian and French governments had more or less agreed to explore the deal. Together, Rome and Paris still controlled 36 percent of ST via France's Areva and France Telecom, and Italy's Finmeccanica.

But the deal never materialized, and ST continued to focus on organic growth and technological partnerships. One such partnership saw the involvement of none other than Motorola, which together with Philips and ST, signed an agreement dubbed the Crolles Alli-

---

[6] Deborah Orr, "The Virtual Consolidator," *Forbes Global* 5, no. 21 (2003), p. 28.

[7] Paul Betts, "Pistorio Strives for 'The Dream of his Life,'" *Financial Times*, October 15, 2002, p. 1.

ance for a joint $1.5 billion investment in research. This work would be done in the recently refurbished Crolles plant, which would specialize in the production of 300mm silicon wafers. A fourth unexpected new entry in the Crolles Alliance was TSMC, the Taiwanese colossus that was rapidly becoming the largest chip foundry in the world. TSMC agreed to produce a portion of the semiconductors developed through the research efforts of the original trio.

Initially the agreement was only meant to be between ST and Philips, recalls Joel Hartmann, who set up the deal.

"But Motorola stepped up and asked to be a part of the project. It was a very quick process; we began talking with them in January 2002 and by April we signed. They were so anxious to come on board that they forced our hand a bit in a slightly strange way. Their COO, Billy Walker, showed up unexpectedly in Paris, took a room in the Georges V [a famous five-star hotel near the Champs-Elysées] and told us that he wasn't going to budge until we brought him the contract to sign. It wasn't clear who was going to pay for the hotel, and Walker being there put tremendous pressure on the legal team that was working on the deal. In a few days we ironed out all the details and then there was a small signing ceremony – right at the hotel."

"With Philips and Motorola," Hartmann emphasizes, "we were competing on products, clients, and markets. But we decided that on research, rather than attacking one another, it made more sense to align our technologies and bring TSMC on board too. It was a way to share the cost of technology, and continue to compete on products, design, customer care, and logistics."

Crolles 2 was inaugurated by French President Jacques Chirac, and Prime Minister Lionel Jospin summed up its significance with these words: "This project, which brings together three of the main players in precision electronics, is a formidable opportunity for France, both in terms of technological development and in terms of job creation." All the effort that Noels' Thomson had dedicated to building a solid French semiconductor industry was ancient history.

In the end, Motorola did not land in Silicon Europe. Instead, the company wound up falling apart – a process that drastically reduced the US brand's global weight compared to its golden years. The semi-

conductor division was spun off in 2004, and a new entity took its
place: Freescale Semiconductor. This company, in turn, was swal-
lowed up by the Dutch NXP.

And so a player left the scene that had made history in the field of
chip production. And its star was slowly fading in many of its other
business ventures too. In 2011, Motorola was split into two companies: Motorola Solutions, dedicated to telecommunications technology, and Motorola Mobility, specializing in mobile telephony. The latter enjoyed a brief burst of success in subsequent years thanks to the
RAZR model, but then Motorola Mobility came up against the same
problems that Nokia had in keeping up with Apple and Samsung
in the smartphone sector. In 2011, Motorola Mobility was acquired
and absorbed into a company that at the turn of the century was just
a small startup. But it had later taken advantage of the collapse of
many stars of the dot-com era to grow and become a giant. Its name
was Google.

Passing the torch

Once the dot-com bubble burst and ST survived the fallout, for Pistorio the time had come to pass the torch. Almost 25 years before he
had accepted the challenge from IRI-STET, leaving behind a sure
thing, a secure position with Motorola in Phoenix, in exchange for
an uncertain future. He had returned to Italy to lead a company that
seemed doomed to fail. But now the Sicilian manager and his team
had become a success story, and the company Pistorio was leaving to
his successors was global, innovative, and financially solid. Another
part of the inheritance bequeathed by ST's first CEO was an original
approach to environmental sustainability, and this at a time when
it would take years before public awareness of related issues would
become what it is today. The September 2000 issue of *Electronic Business*[8] crowned Pistorio the "environmental evangelist," outlining the
rules the company had already set down for itself in the 1990s. At

---

[8] John Kador, "Environmental Evangelist. For Pasquale Pistorio, the chips
he's playing are green," *Electronic Business* (September 2000), p. 72.

that point – years ahead of nearly the whole business world – ST embarked on a journey, and the final destination was to make all its production activities carbon neutral. The deadline for reaching this goal is now 2027, ahead of the entire sector, thanks to ongoing efforts that began a quarter of a century ago.

Pistorio compiled an ecological handbook for ST and encouraged all his employees to come up with ideas and processes that would allow the company to recycle and produce sustainably, as far as possible. This approach actually took shape around the family dinner table. It was actually his son Carmelo who prompted Pistorio to reflect on the environmental sustainability of ST's industrial activities. That made Carmelo a forebear, in a sense, to the future Greta Thunberg generation. "He challenged some of the values – or, I should say, lack of values – of the industrial group I represented," Pistorio told *Electronic Business*. "He told me that if I was serious about making our business model work for the benefit of humanity, the company should commit to environmentally sustainable development."

For Pistorio's generation – and for many other leading figures who grew up during the pioneering years of the microchip – it was time to step back and make room for the talented young people the company had cultivated. To find someone to take his place, Pistorio looked inside ST to promote a person from his team, and then offered a shortlist of candidates to the Supervisory Board. The Board accepted the idea of an internal promotion and selected Carlo Bozotti to take the roles of President and CEO, while Alain Dutheil was tapped to be the new COO. Between them, Bozotti and Dutheil[9] tallied up over 60 years of experience in the semiconductor field. They had both

[9] Born in the south of France, Dutheil earned a degree in Engineering from the École Supérieure d'Ingénieurs in Marseilles. He started working in 1969 at Texas Instruments and in 1983 he joined Thomson Semiconducteurs where he was manager of the Aix-en-Provence plant. After having served as general manager of the Discreet Division, in 1989 he became Corporate VP for all the manufacturing assembly and testing activities of STMicroelectronics. To this role was subsequently added the position of Corporate VP for Human Resources. This latter position he continued to hold even after he was assigned the role of Corporate VP for Strategic Planning in 1994.

dedicated their entire professional careers to this sector, a span of time that covered the greater part of the history of the microelectronics industry.

The decision was announced in March 2004, one year ahead of the annual shareholders meeting where the new CEO would be approved. The passing of the torch happened smoothly because there was no obligation to alternate between Italian and French executives; the primary focus instead was on the professional background of the candidate.

The new CEO had climbed the entire corporate ladder, first at SGS and then at ST, and he started from the lowest rung as an apprentice. Bozotti was born in 1952 in Noviglio (between Milan and Pavia), and he went to SGS-ATES to complete his university thesis in electronic engineering: developing a mathematical model for a bipolar power transistor.[10] Later he was hired in 1977 to work in the power applications lab of Castelletto.

> "For some time, I dreamed of continuing to do pure research," Bozotti says, "and instead I ended up counting transistors in a warehouse in Catania. I had just started working in the company and they sent me to our Catania factory. Among other things, it was the first time I had ever boarded an airplane. I had to compile a statistic on certain types of transistors that were buried in a mountain of boxes. I remember having had the outlandish idea of asking if I could borrow a forklift to move the boxes and the warehouse manager got furious with this kid who was giving him trouble."

A few years after Pistorio joined the company, Bozotti was promoted to product manager for the telecommunications, computer peripherals, and automotive sectors. After the merger between SGS and Thomson, he became director of strategic marketing and key customers, and he was later sent to the US to run ST's operations there.

Seemingly forewarning the challenges that Bozotti would have to face the moment he became CEO, a blackout blanketed nearly the whole of New England just as Bozotti arrived with his fami-

---

[10] He earned his degree from the University of Pavia.

ly in Boston in 1991. This was caused by what would go down in history as the Perfect Storm,[11] which pummeled the Atlantic coast. A rare meteorological phenomenon – an Atlantic hurricane merged with other storms – created a catastrophic severe weather event that wreaked death and destruction along the Eastern seaboard of the US. Many coastal communities were hit hard, including Kennebunkport, Maine, where the then US president, George Bush Sr., had a summer home.

Bozotti was a big soccer fan, and he and his two sons did their part to raise the bar on the quality of that sport in Boston's schools. But more importantly, he managed to triple ST's sales in the US, the market that Silicon Europe had always set its sights on. Revenues surged from $300 million to $1 billion. Upon returning to Europe after three years in the US, he was tasked with heading up sales and marketing in Europe, as well as handling global strategic marketing and major clients and partnerships. Then he was appointed head of the ST's memory products group, before becoming Pistorio's heir.

At the annual shareholders meeting on March 17, 2005, Bozotti's appointment as CEO was made official. In his new role, he began to follow the strategic roadmap that he had drawn up with Dutheil and the new leadership team. ST had not yet recovered the financial performance of the pre-dot-com bubble period. As Bozotti says: "Some things had changed; the market wasn't growing like it used to. Fabless models were gaining ground. Our competitors were operating without factories, delegating production to Asian manufacturers and abandoning the integrated model that was the basis for the sector's success. What's more, the euro-dollar exchange rate had taken a dive, which had a huge negative impact on our books." It's hard to underestimate the repercussions of the currency fluctuations in the 2000s on the financial performance of European companies with global markets such as ST. At its low point, the euro was worth $0.83 in 2001; it peaked at $1.60 in 2008, in the midst of the financial crisis.

---

[11] *The Perfect Storm* became famous thanks to a book by Sebastian Junger published in 1997; it later became a 2000 movie starring George Clooney, a box office hit.

Bozotti and his team responded by first optimizing production. "We made the company 'lighter' on assets," Bozotti explains. "We closed various modules and production sites, integrating and rationalizing activities. Next, we had to transform the new Crolles plant from a research center into an integrated R&D and mass production facility. And we decided to start a new module in Agrate to mass produce our MEMS."

The point of these sacrifices was to shield and shore up research. As Bozotti remembers:

> "We put in the effort to reinforce some of the areas we were leading in, focusing on complete solutions for the automotive market in particular, with new digital platforms for car navigation, Advanced Driver Assistance Systems (ADAS), and 32-bit microcontrollers for so-called under the hood applications. As for these microcontrollers, we decided to concentrate on 32 bits, going directly from the 8-bit product family to 32 bits, leapfrogging 16 bits. Finally, we also set our sights on solutions for the consumer electronics market, stepping up development of smartphone application processors. For this last market, we also wanted to find a partner for the 4G modem, which we didn't have."

An ST product line that didn't bode well as far as market success was nonvolatile NOR flash memory,[12] which couldn't store the large amounts of data that NAND flash memory could. But this was a technology ST didn't have, and developing and industrializing it would take massive R&D and use extremely capital-intensive production lines. The resources necessary to make a serious incursion into this sector were totally out of reach.

Bozotti decided to make a drastic move: a joint venture in NOR with Intel, ST's eternal rival. "The deal with Intel allowed us to de-consolidate our nonvolatile memory business, move the engineers that had been working on that research, and convert the factories in Catania and Agrate to BCD, extending their lifespans by at least 30 years." Bozotti continues, "It was a painful decision, but it turned out

---

[12] A type of product used for storing BIOS, the program used by microprocessors to boot up a computer after powering it on, for example.

well and it allowed Agrate and Catania to continue to be the crown jewels they still are today."

All these initiatives allowed ST to weather the "perfect storm" of 2008 and 2009, which was actually the confluence of two storms: the euro-dollar exchange rate and the great global recession that followed the collapse of Lehman Brothers. Yet through all this, ST's financial solidity was never jeopardized, and the company ended the decade with success and big ambitions for the future. But success and ambition aside, Bozotti had to contend with a situation where another perfect storm was brewing.

And this one was the most difficult and dangerous of them all.

The smartphone crisis

In 2005 and 2006, the whole world witnessed an unusual phenomenon. For more than a decade, tens of billions of people had been carrying around phones in their pockets, but suddenly they were no longer called "cellphones" but "smartphones." For some time, it wasn't clear what made smartphones smart, and there was a great deal of experimentation going on to find out. The most common conception of a smartphone was initially something very much like the products launched by the Canadian company Research in Motion (RIM). First and foremost, the Blackberry. Initially a pager was the added value with respect to traditional phones; later came messaging and calendar functions. In addition, the hugely popular BlackBerry keyboard allowed users to send emails and do (limited) Internet searches. At the time, this was seen as the formula for success.

The evolution in cellphones also led to giving them bigger screens and, for the first time, enabling them to take pictures. Nokia, Motorola, and Ericsson followed this path, developing proprietary operating systems as RIM had done, while keeping the basic design and layout of traditional phones. Others tried different options, such as the American company Palm, which put its money on an explosion in demand for handheld computers, or Palm Pilots.

All this maneuvering was practically nullified on January 9, 2007, when Steve Jobs took the stage during the Macworld convention, at San Francisco's Moscone Center. From the pocket of his jeans, he took out the first ever iPhone. Suddenly, everything else was old news, and the smartphone found its archetype. It was an object made of aluminum, glass, and black plastic; it came with a touch screen and no keyboard. And it immediately presented as a second, pocket-sized identity that offered users multiple functions: They could make phone calls, surf the internet, listen to music, take photos, send emails, update their calendars, and much more.

A short time before, Facebook had come online. This social network had been invented on a university campus, and at first was only used by students, but in September 2006 global access was opened. And at the same time, an extremely powerful, revolutionary web-based messaging service came on the scene and rapidly accumulated a global user base: Twitter.

On October 9, 2006, Google announced that it was entering the world of video by purchasing a service created just a year before for over $1.5 billion. The three guys who invented it wanted to have an easy way to share a video that everyone was clamoring to see: Janet Jackson's wardrobe malfunction at the Super Bowl. (During a duet with Justin Timberlake, he tore off part of her costume, accidentally revealing her breast.) The three computer whizzes named their invention YouTube.

So, over the two-year period from 2006 to 2008, the digital world went to warp speed with the debut of the iPhone, Facebook, Twitter, and YouTube. At the same time, blogs and Google searches exploded, Google News rocked the news world, the open source programming model burst on the scene (which Google itself relied on to launch its Android operating system in response to Apple), digital photography technology took a giant leap forward, and many other innovations were launched. And all this was followed by the US stock market crash triggered by the collapse of Lehman Brothers and the subprime mortgage crisis, which led to a global recession.

More than a perfect storm, it was a monster storm, and it left many casualties in its wake. In the telephony sector, some companies were quick to read the writing on the wall. Google, for example, absorbed the knowhow of Motorola and developed android architecture. A number of players recognized its potential and snatched it up to use as an operating system, as was the case of Samsung. Others clung to the past, held back by a corporate culture that was incapable of embracing change, convinced that they could defend proprietary systems and architectures. That two-year period marked the beginning of the end for these companies; RIM-BlackBerry was one, and Nokia was another.

"Nokia for us wasn't just a storm, it was a tsunami that started in 2011, the year of the real tsunami in Japan," Bozotti recalls. "It happened when Nokia's new leadership decided to abruptly cut off funding for their proprietary operating system and replace it with Windows instead of running with Android." Even though Nokia looked rock solid – in the third quarter of 2007 it had just attained a record-breaking global mobile phone market share of 40.4 percent – the Finnish company started losing sizeable chunks of this share after the smartphone revolution. The iPhone at the time only had 5 percent of the market, but it was starting to take off, together with Samsung's smartphones. At the end of 2010, Nokia's global market share was still 30 percent, with a strong presence in Europe and Asia, but the new strategy failed and in the span of just a few fiscal quarters, the market leader imploded. Its telephony business was subsequently acquired by Microsoft, marking the end of Europe's presence in this enormous market.

In 2009, ST had set up a joint venture with another major telephony player, Ericsson. The goal was technological leadership in all the chips that make smartphones work, including the digital heart of the telephone (adding Ericsson's modem to ST's internally developed application processor). The customer portfolio of the newly created ST-Ericsson included Nokia, Samsung and the selfsame Sony Ericsson. The products were linked to power management, radio frequency, and the digital heart of the cellphone we mentioned above. These would have continued to be a solid business were it not for the serious crisis in mobile telephony that first hit Nokia and then Ericsson. Instead, Apple and Samsung were becoming integrated enterprises, so gradually they were handling all their chip production in-house. In 2012, it was time to shelve the partnership with Ericsson too, and ST was forced to contend with the repercussions of the crisis its clients and partners were experiencing.

"If we combine Nokia and Sony Ericsson, we lost $2.7 billion, almost one-third of our turnover," recalls Bozotti, who was at the time dealing with a major predicament. "ST's revenues took a nosedive, from $10 billion in 2011, we dropped to $7 billion in 2015, our worst year."

Joel Hartmann can still picture the scene many years before at Carrollton, in Texas, where he was sent to try to repurpose the shuttered Mostek factory. It had gone bankrupt after betting everything on one customer.

"With Nokia's collapse," he explains, "there was some internal debate around the need to stop production at Crolles, where 90 percent of the fab's 200mm output was earmarked for Nokia. It was a total shock for us to see our number one customer's turnover crater, from two billion dollars to zero in just three years. At Crolles … all our experience and everything we had created was called into question. It was a really tough time."

Recovery

"At the end of 2012, when we announced that the joint venture with Ericsson was over, it put paid to our ambition to become a global market leader in smartphones with solutions that integrated the digital heart of the phone," Bozotti recollects. But Silicon Europe had been built over decades; the Crolles-Grenoble district in particular was specialized in imaging, as well as the digital side of MEMS and many other digital products. So not even a blow as heavy as this would knock them down. "We had to have the courage to react with determination and turn this defeat into a great opportunity," explains Bozotti.

There was no need to sell off production facilities because plants had already been completely optimized.

"We decided instead to reallocate all our invaluable engineering resources, people who had been working on application processors and some other smartphone products, and move them over to microcontrollers, automotive platforms, new imaging solutions, and ASIC products in FD-SOI. To accomplish this, my second-in-command Jean-Marc

Chery took over all the company's embedded processing and imaging. It was a terribly demanding experience, but a fundamental one for him. We had some extremely trying times, the effort was massive, but it paid off tremendously: ST recovered, and from 2016 on started growing again more and more rapidly, sustainably, and profitably. And this still continues today."

One of the most complicated stages in that process was when ST decided to pull out of the segments of wireless connection devices and set-top boxes, the range of external equipment that added functions to televisions, monitors, and video projectors. A popular example that we are all familiar with is the decoder, which enabled TVs to access satellite transmissions, digital terrestrial signals, and various pay-per-view services. France had a long manufacturing tradition of set-top boxes, going back to the time when the French semiconductor industry was mainly focused on television.

There was strong resistance and pressure on top management to stop ST from abandoning set-top boxes. But Bozotti and his future successor Chery asserted their decision-making autonomy regarding the company's industrial strategies and forged ahead, shutting down production of these chips to go even further to concentrate engineering resources on what they considered key product families. A total of some 2,500 engineers were moved from wireless devices and set-top boxes to other units.

Another French area of expertise proved to be a potent weapon to bring to bear in the Nokia crisis: the production of microcontrollers, a crown jewel of Silicon Europe that would become even more precious. Carmelo Papa signed a partnership with ARM, headquartered in Cambridge (in Britain) to obtain a license for the use of the eponymous and powerful British architecture on ST microcontrollers. These would become the core of the Italian-French devices. In 2007, Bozotti tasked Claude Dardanne with coordinating the business, disseminating the products, and growing the software and applications ecosystem, with the aim of reaching tens of thousands of new clients. In no time, sales surged and the payoff was explosive.

Demand for microcontrollers came from a wide range of industries, from automotive to telephony. But at the start of the new century smart cards were where the action was. ST's minuscule electronic brains were controlling credit cards, company badges, IDs, and countless other applications. All entrusted to those little chip-embedded rectangles of plastic that fill our wallets today. For decades, as we have seen, Roland Moreno's invention was exclusively a French phenomenon. But now in the twenty-first century, this technology started spreading all over the world.

"When I took the reins on our microcontroller production in 2007," Dardanne says, "we were working on 8-bit, 16-bit and 32-bit devices. So we rationalized production and focused on 32 bits, which became our basic product. Then we shored up the team, transferring the engineers who came from ST-Ericsson or from set-top box production to the microcontroller unit. And we saw the results over the years. In 2007, our microcontrollers had a 2.4 percent global market share worth $700 to $800 million. Today we have about 20 percent to 25 percent of the market, a share that's worth $3.3 billion."

After playing catch-up for years in a sector once dominated by Motorola, in 2022 ST took the top spot in the world in general-purpose microcontrollers, which are everywhere now: in household appliances, in digitized industrial manufacturing processes, in wireless connectivity devices, and in many other areas related to the IoT. Microcontrollers are actually much more than simple chips. In a way, these highly complex little brains are the building blocks of artificial intelligence. Winning the top spot in the world in this arena shows just how far Silicon Europe had come since the early days when research was getting underway at LETI in the 1970s.

Silicon Europe faced the perfect storm of the smartphone crisis, and came out on the other side by tapping a deep pool of internal resources, and making painful choices and strategic decisions. One example is a larger presence on the Chinese market, where ST has a sizeable assembly plant in Shenzhen.

Along with all these initiatives, it is interesting to see how in its efforts to compensate for what was lost with Nokia, ST found itself playing a key role as a partner and supplier to the company that had sparked off the entire crisis: Apple. The Cupertino company had already worked with Silicon Europe in the past, thanks to Steve Jobs's philosophy to search the world for exceptional technology to use in Apple's products. The firm's innovation hunters certainly took note of what the Italians and French managed to do with MEMS, and when the Americans wanted to add gyroscopes and accelerometers to their phones, it was inevitable that they would reach out to technical experts in Europe.

At that time, Jobs was launching new versions of the iPhone along with the first tablet – the iPad – which debuted in 2010. All these devices needed an easy and efficient way to rotate what was displayed on their screens, switching from vertical to horizontal. They also had to be equipped with sensors that transformed external analog inputs into digital (for popular functions on today's smartphones such as pedometers, for example).

MEMS were ideal for this kind of thing, so Carmelo Papa flew to Cupertino to present them to Apple. During a meeting, as he was reassuring the American managers that ST's supply chain was solid, and outlining all the procedures that would be put in place to guarantee product quality, Steve Jobs unexpectedly showed up.

"I remember him walking into the room with that gangly gait of his and the scruffy beard," Papa recalls. "They told him who I was and why I was there. He knew exactly what our products were for. He looked at me, pointed his finger, and with his typical abrupt tone, told me: 'Hey, this thing is really important for us, if you mess anything up, you won't set foot in this building again for the next fifteen years.' I replied: 'Fifteen years? That doesn't bother me.' 'Why not?' 'Because by then I'll be retired!' It took him a beat, and then said: 'Oh, I like this guy.' He shook my hand hard and warned me: 'You better behave!' and then he left."

ST did behave, and earned the trust of Apple's top management. It was the start of a working relationship encompassing a number of technologies and a range of products that continues to this day. (The US company is one of the top ten clients for the French-Italian company.)

The French experience in imaging proved to be critical too. At Crolles, they had been working for years to develop cameras for Nokia's cellphones, which functioned thanks to the CMOS sensors that controlled the image capture processes. When Nokia left the scene and the curtain came up on the current smartphone era – dominated by Apple, Samsung, Oppo, Xiaomi, and Huawei[13] – the battle of the megapixels for RBG cameras intensified, but the competition shifted to other imaging spheres as well. Examples are Time of Flight services and applications for global shutter sensors. As we've seen during our visits to ST's research hubs in France, for decades in and around Grenoble, experts have been studying photons and sensors in relation to the speed of light. The technologies they've developed as a result help Apple's phones do many things, to include face recognition.

It's an inspiring story of collaboration between Silicon Europe and Silicon Valley, and it's continuing today and growing even stronger. But as is always the case, it wasn't exactly a walk in the park. "In 2006 we began exploring ways to realize in CMOS the devices used for Time of Flight processes for smartphones. It took seven years to complete development, overcoming endless technical problems and challenges," recalls Aussedat, head of the Imaging business at ST. "There were times when we considered stopping everything and abandoning our research, but we stuck it out. And Apple rewarded us by choosing us."

The crisis that lasted from 2008 to 2015 ultimately strengthened Silicon Europe. ST emerged as a global company that sloughed off its weaker business activities to concentrate on a vast range of areas of excellence. A winning decision was to continue investing in research and development, come what may. This is what has enabled the firm to successfully rise to the challenges of a market that evolves at lightning-fast speed.

Navigating all the "perfect storms" that the market kept churning up, Bozotti steered ST's production toward certain areas that were firmly established and tightly linked to the traditions of Silicon Europe. One technological block consisted of MEMS sensors and their various iterations. Then there was smart power, with BCD and simi-

---

[13] Thanks to ST's knowhow, in recent years the company started a collaboration with Huawei too. However, this was interrupted when sanctions were imposed against the Chinese company in 2019 by the US and most Western countries.

lar products, which could combine logic, analog, and power functions on one chip. Next, imaging sensors and the entire imaging technology unit, based in France. Plus, CMOS products and extremely low-dissipation and resistance applications based on FD-SOI. And finally, embedded logic technologies (CMOS loaded with nonvolatile memory) for microcontrollers.

It was an impressive technology portfolio, and another innovation would soon be added.

This time, Made in Catania.

12   Catania, Where Silicon Still Surprises

Stardust

While ST was facing the darkest years of the crisis, between 2008 and 2015, there was a new growing awareness around the dangers the environment was facing. Living a sustainable existence in which our daily routines no longer threaten the survival of the planet's ecosystem: this is the greatest challenge of the 21st century. In 2015, the UN set down 17 Sustainable Development Goals (SDGs), with the overarching aim of decarbonizing all human activity in all member states by 2030. The SDGs cover a broad range of economic and social issues, but in many of them what appears as either a central or peripheral theme is mobility.

Whether it's about moving cargo or people, mobility is one of the tests that will determine whether we are making a real effort to respond to the environmental crisis or whether we are failing. The undisputed champion of this gigantic, planet-wide test is the electric car. Moving beyond the era of the internal combustion engine is now considered an inescapable goal. But how and when this will happen is the topic of constant debate among scientists, institutions, and the world of production.

The success of electric mobility is contingent on an efficient, extensive recharging infrastructure, as well as devices that allow vehicles to charge quickly, and store and convert electricity efficiently. Energy storage is the buzzword, especially as it relates to raw materials such as lithium that latest-generation batteries need. But energy conversion and anything having to do with fast charging are equally challenging issues.

Lithium batteries produce direct current (DC), but electric vehicles (EVs) are built with power units that use alternate current (AC), which is much more efficient. This is where inverters come into play. These devices transform direct current into alternate current, and they depend once again on an essential ingredient: silicon, a material we have got to know very well on our voyage of discovery of semiconductors. But the revolution in this field can be attributed to silicon's younger cousin. The killer application for electric vehicles is, in fact, a material containing both silicon and carbon. It's emerging as a great ally of electric mobility, and a critical force in the battle humanity is waging against CO_2 emissions: silicon carbide (molecular formula: SiC). And the place where the most advanced production methods for this material are being developed is ST's historic Catania plant, the company's center of excellence for power electronics.

To fully understand what silicon carbide is doing for electric mobility, and what it promises to do even more in the future (not to mention all the vital applications in the industrial sector, and recently in aeronautics and space as well), we need to go back in time. The year was 1824 when Jöns Jacob Berzelius, a Swedish chemist, proposed the idea that a carbon-silicon compound could exist in nature. But the first evidence to corroborate this theory didn't come until 1892, when the American chemist Edward G. Acheson was attempting to create an artificial diamond. By heating a mixture of carbon-coke and silicon to a high temperature, he forged a crystal that was as hard as a diamond, but different in nature. Acheson hypothesized it was a carbon-aluminum bond, which he called *carborundum*, to indicate that the hardness of this new synthetic material was halfway between corundum (A1203) and carbon. This discovery paved the way for large-scale production of silicon carbide for the abrasives industry, for which it was originally intended.

Silicon carbide appeared to be a compound that could only be produced in a laboratory, but the following year, future French Nobel laureate Henri-Ferdinand Moissan discovered an infinitesimal quantity of the material in a meteorite in Canyon Diablo, Arizona. In honor of the discoverer, the material was called *moissanite*. Later studies proved that moissanite is the natural version of what we call silicon carbide, a material that is extremely rare on Earth but extremely common in space, especially in meteors. So we can say that in his lab, Acheson created a kind of stardust resembling a diamond. It would take years before all its other qualities would be fully revealed, but today these qualities make silicon carbide a revolutionary component for power semiconductor devices.

A substance that falls from heaven, but only in minuscule quantities, which is why today it is produced almost exclusively in the lab. During the 20th century, thanks to its exceptional hardness, this material became an extremely powerful abrasive; it has also been used to produce the ceramic plates that line bullet-proof vests and the protective shields on space telescopes. But silicon carbide had something more to offer and that something was revealed in semiconductor research centers: it reduces energy dispersion to a surprising extent. One of the effects of which is that it vastly accelerates electricity transfer processes, such as the ones used to charge electric vehicles.

In 1955, Jan Anthony Lely obtained pure silicon carbide crystals in the allotropic form 6H-SiC using a sublimation method that took his name. The potential use of this material as a semiconductor arose in the 1960s, but was limited to academic circles owing to the difficulty in obtaining pure, monocrystalline substances. From 1978 to 1981, Tairov and Tsvetkov invented a replicable method for growing monocrystalline SiC ingots based on a sublimation process. They began with a monocrystalline seed of ultra-pure SiC in ideal conditions and at a controlled temperature using a process which they dubbed the Modified Lely Method.[1] Then in 1989, Baliga[2] proposed using SiC as the basic semiconducting material for manufacturing power units.

---

[1] Yuri M. Tairov and Valeri F. Tsvetkov, "Investigation of Growth Processes of Ingots of Silicon Carbide Single Crystals," *Journal of Crystal Growth* 43, no. 2 (1978), pp. 209–12.

[2] Bantval J. Baliga, "Power Semiconductor Device Figure of Merit for High-Frequency Applications," *IEEE Electron Device Letters* 10, no. 10 (1989), pp. 455–57.

Silicon-based inverters or DC-to-AC converters have much greater dispersion and power loss, which means less efficiency in electric mobility. What silicon carbide can do is cut charging time (for example, from one hour to half an hour or less), and decrease the overall cost of a single electric vehicle by somewhere in the range of $2,000 per model, thanks to the efficiencies this substance can offer. Another plus would be a smaller battery pack to cover average mileage. All this explains why a Goldman Sachs study predicts a boom in the silicon carbide industry.

And today Catania can claim the title of world capital of silicon carbide production for power semiconductor devices.

Transistor 4.0

To understand how silicon carbide is revolutionizing electric mobility, let's return to the topic of power applications, starting from the device we encountered at the beginning of our journey: the transistor. The bipolar transistor invented in Bell Labs by Shockley, Bardeen, and Brattain was an electronic device with three terminals (base, emitter, and collector). By modulating the current that enters the base, the transistor can be used as both a power amplifier as well as an on/off switch to open and close electronic circuits. From the outset, this type of transistor was used in industry, consumer electronics, and the automotive sector. But soon enough bipolar technology could no longer satisfy the requirements of more advanced technologies. Internet-era applications, for instance, called for more efficient transistors.

An initial breakthrough, as we've seen, was the MOSFET transistor, characterized by a conduction mechanism that only activates with unipolar charges. MOSFET makes it possible to handle higher frequency applications, which go beyond the scope of the original transistor. MOSFET is also utilized in emerging technologies, for example, the IoT, robotics, home automation, smart cities, and in the automotive sector.

Over time, a third type of transistor was developed, the Insulated Gate Bipolar Transistor (IGBT), which in a sense is a bipolar/MOSFET hybrid. Although it is not optimal for middle to high frequencies, it is very competitive in terms of cost and performance.[3] With the advent of silicon carbide, now it was possible to use this material to build a MOSFET transistor: hence the name SiC MOSFET.

The SiC MOSFET, the latest character to appear in the story of the transistor (the cornerstone of the modern power electronics industry in its entirety), combines the simplicity of MOSFET control on voltage and IGBT with unipolar conduction. It also handles very high frequencies effectively, which would be unthinkable for any other type of transistor. What's more, it can reach a high operating voltage (between 650 and 2,200V and above), and it is unrivalled in applications where high efficiency is essential. The SiC MOSFET is even well behaved in environments that reach high temperatures; examples include many industrial processes, and applications in the automotive and telecommunications sectors. And when it comes to managing inverters (for energy production from solar cells or batteries in electric cars), it's unbeatable, not to mention very competitive in terms of costs and performance.

In light of all this, it's not surprising that the SiC MOSFET is considered a true enabler of the mobility transformation as we transition from hydrocarbon to electric power. In Catania, studies on silicon carbide and its properties began more than 20 years ago. Here too the approach to research, as with imaging applications, was similar to what LETI did for Grenoble in semiconductors. At the University of Catania and at the local headquarters of the National Research Council (in Italian, CNR), a research stream was initiated specializing in silicon carbide, thanks to close collaboration with ST. After several years of research, in 2004 the first SiC-based diodes were produced; then in 2009 came the first MOSFET transistors, which went into mass production in 2014. This coincided with the jump start of

----

[3] The IGBT is a device with three terminals (a gate, an emitter, and a collector) which resembles both the MOSFET (as regards control on voltage through the gate) and the bipolar transistor (as far as output, with the conduction channel created by electrons and holes). The optimal range of use for an IGBT is between 200 and 2,200V, in other words, it can handle a wide variety of power applications, from industrial (welders, control motors, etc.) to all the high-tension telecom applications.

the electric car industry, "driven" mainly by a US company that was destined to become one of ST's key clients: Tesla.

"There were some meetings with Elon Musk, one in particular when I went to visit their Gigafactory in Nevada," Bozotti recollects. "They wanted to upgrade the efficiency of their power applications. The aim was to work on the traction inverter, and silicon carbide turned out to be the solution they were looking for. They even developed new assembly-line techniques to minimize dissipation and cut down on weight, extending the driving range." ST came on board Tesla's Model 3 project and continued collaborating with that company on other models and industrial sectors as well.

Silicon carbide was proof positive of a successful strategy. On one hand, it enabled ST to streamline its assets to give the company more agility in meeting market challenges, and on the other, it kept the bar high on research. And research, since the days of SGS and Thomson, has proven to be Silicon Europe's secret weapon. Bozotti confirms this: "We invested in research and development in Catania, like we did at Agrate for MEMS and at Crolles with a major expansion in 300mm wafer production on new digital technologies. In other words, we never stopped investing, even when situations like the Nokia incident created problems for us. And that made all the difference." But even when a company leans in to research, you still need ideas and – more importantly – the people to make them happen. And sometimes, you need to twist some arms. Which is what Carmelo Papa did in Catania to fast-track silicon carbide research.

"We started mulling this over about 20 years ago," Papa recollects. "And to make headway with research, as always, you need to experiment a bit, get your hands dirty, mess around, as I like to say. Except to do that [with silicon carbide], you had to use extremely expensive instruments. In particular, we needed an epitaxial reactor that cost €6 million. I asked Bozotti if we could buy one, but back then we were trying to cut costs and tighten our belt, and it is no small thing to request such an expenditure for pure research. So I told Carlo we needed it for the transistor production that was already underway. He knew what I was up to, so he asked me if we also needed it to research silicon carbide. 'A llittle … maybe a bit more than a little,' I answered. And he let me buy it."

The development of silicon carbide semiconductors in Catania was far from a simple undertaking. Papa remembers the initial obstacles, mostly arising from defects in the devices. That was inevitable with a new technology, until you had all the knowhow you needed to manage the processes correctly. Even the cost of the devices was too high at first. But gradually all the problems were resolved, setting in motion a new cycle of power semiconductor production in Silicon Europe. The devices that drove this new cycle were capable of reaching high – even extremely high – voltage, which is needed in some industrial production processes. And the chips were much smaller than standard.

The success of silicon carbide also coincides with the successful relaunch of ST's Catania plant, which was certainly not a given in the days of SGS-ATES. Papa was there for all the milestones along the way for the Sicilian production facility. Here's what he has to say:

"The new life of Catania springs from Pistorio's decision, back in the day, to turn this assembly-only factory into something different. I remember him telling me that in the beginning, Catania was losing 117 percent of its revenues: for every 100 we produced and sold, we were losing 117. Looking at the numbers alone, we were better off closing shop and sending everybody home. But Pistorio realized that it made no sense to work on assembly when globalization was already creating low-cost production opportunities elsewhere. What we needed was research and development. So he revolutionized the factory, and even leveled up the skillset of the work force: at the time, there were many workers who hadn't even finished elementary school. Now he started hiring exclusively high school and college graduates. Then there was the collaboration with the university and the CNR. And very gradually, this changed the face of Catania."

Today, ST is the heart of Etna Valley, a driver of local innovation that will be even more powerful when the new factory currently under construction in Catania goes online. This will expand silicon carbide wafer production capacity, switching from the current 150mm diameter wafers to 200mm. With SiC production in Singapore too, Silicon Europe is gaining ground in the race to support the transition to electric mobility. Since 2017, when large-scale production of silicon carbide began in Catania with second generation SiC MOSFETs, ST has supplied the automotive industry with over 200 million devices. Production capacity increased two and a half times between 2020 and 2022 and it will double again by 2025.

But scientific research into semiconductors is never-ending, and hunting season is already open for new materials. The journey that began in the 1950s with germanium devices continued to the era of silicon, the enabler of the digital revolution of the last few decades. The next stop was silicon carbide, with Silicon Europe blazing the trail and garnering expertise along the way. But the path doesn't end here.

There is another semiconductor that is stealing the spotlight.

De bello gallico – On the Gallic War[4]

In 1875, French chemist Paul-Émile Lecoq de Boisbaudran, studying samples of minerals taken from the Pyrenees, detected a material that had all the characteristics of a new element. He called it gallium, paying tribute to the name the ancient Romans gave to present-day France. But gallium, like germanium and silicon, dozed quietly on the periodic table, waiting around for someone to figure out what to do with it. Some chemical compounds made with the element (such as gallium arsenide) had captured the attention of electronics researchers in the 1980s because they have high electron mobility. But among the compounds formed with de Boisbaudran's discovery, the real star of the show only took the stage in the 1990s: gallium nitride (GaN).

One of the first people to recognize its potential was Shuji Nakamura, an American electronic engineer of Japanese descent. In 1993, he presented a gallium nitride light-emitting diode (LED) device that emitted blue light – a real breakthrough for the lighting industry. This was a building block that was used to construct the entire LED industry as we know it today, revolutionizing light bulbs by making them more efficient and sustainable. For his research into

---

[4] Julius Caesar's personal account of the Gallic Wars.

blue-light-emitting GaN diodes, Nakamura won the 2014 Nobel prize in physics (with Isamu Akasaki and Hiroshi Amano).

Nakamura's studies piqued interest in GaN thanks to its hardness and its electrical properties. Extensive studies began in the semiconductor industry, revealing that GaN is another compound that holds great promise for the future. Here too Silicon Europe is taking the lead, spearheaded by LETI in Grenoble, where research has been underway for many years.

> "Like silicon carbide," explains Papa, who led this research before he retired, "gallium nitride has a wide forbidden band or band gap,[5] but it also has characteristics that allow us to use it in integrated circuits, unlike SiC. This technology may have a brilliant future because not only can it handle extremely high voltage like silicon carbide, but you can also make integrated circuits, and in the future even complex circuits. So we're not talking about single circuit transistors alone, but integrated circuits made of a new material – no longer silicon – that may open the door to countless new uses."

The potential applications for GaN are vast: from the automotive to the space industry, from the IoT to consumer electronics. (There are already gallium nitride battery chargers for smartphones that are smaller and more efficient than the ones that use silicon semiconductors.) And on this front too Silicon Europe has been playing offense for many years. The ST factory leading the way in this case is the French facility in Tours, where a pilot production scheme has been activated and a new manufacturing plant is under construction for 200mm wafers in gallium nitride.

As Catania and Tours show, the greatest challenge for ST was to keep up research efforts on all these fronts even during the most turbulent years of Bozotti's leadership, which came to a head from 2013 to 2015, before solutions gradually emerged.

---

[5] The band gap or forbidden band in a semiconductor is the range of energy in which no electrons exist; it is used to measure and classify various materials based on their electronic characteristics.

"In 2016 and 2017, new programs got underway with Apple," Bozotti says. "Then various projects in the automotive industry picked up speed, like with Tesla. And there was continuing collaboration with Mobileye on projects for ADAS – Advanced Driver Assistance Systems, and research initiatives on self-driving vehicles have started multiplying. All sectors which need increasingly complex chips, and we've added them to our traditional activities. Our STM32 microcontrollers are everywhere now, the choice of tens of thousands of clients all over the world, the heart of an infinity of IoT applications."

New markets, new clients, intense research, and shoring up production in areas where Silicon Europe's leadership was already consolidated: this is what allowed ST to emerge stronger than ever from crises such as the one set off by Nokia, and start back again on the path of growth.

And on this path, the time had come to pass the baton a second time since the Italian-French merger.

And once more, the honor would go to a home-grown talent.

13 A Smart Future

In the eye of the storm

The extremely complicated start of the 2020s, with the pandemic, the globalization crisis, and new war zones, made Jean-Marc Chery a very busy and very sought-after man. Here he is in November 2021: "Old and new clients are calling me, companies large and small, they're ringing me on my mobile – even late at night – and they're all saying the same thing: 'We need semiconductors.'" Walking briskly through ST's Geneva headquarters with his shirt sleeves rolled up, there was no hint of satisfaction or smugness in his words. For the CEO of a company such as ST, a boom in demand for products, as happened in 2021–22, should have been gratifying. But Chery knew that the answer to many of those phone calls, often from long-standing customers, wouldn't be affirmative, simply because the world was suddenly facing a shortage of semiconductors, with no way to cut corners on the time it takes to meet the excess demand.

The global slowdown of 2020 (the first year of the COVID-19 pandemic) brought production to a standstill in some sectors, and consequently orders dried up too. Then the world got back to business faster than expected, while there was still total chaos in logistics. What's more, the virus kept coming back in waves, causing continual closings and reopenings. The global boom in smart working fueled the rising demand for consumer electronics, PCs, printers – all products that function thanks to semiconductors. The automotive sector too, another gigantic client for semiconductors, raced to make up for lost time, with car dealership lots practically empty. Growth was explosive in the semiconductor industry, to include economic growth, as we have seen. But for ST and the other big players, keeping up with demand was proving extremely complicated. Then came the war in Ukraine, inflation, and new closures in China prompted by the pandemic. In 2023, normal was still a long way off for the semiconductor industry, and Chery's life continued to be complicated.

Since 2018, when he took over as President and CEO of ST, the past three years have been the most critical time for Chery, critical yet brimming with interesting prospects. On May 12, 2022, while meeting investors and analysts in Paris for the company's Capital Markets Day, Chery forecast revenues hitting $15 billion for that year. But he didn't stop there. For the first time he presented his grand ambition: to take ST over the $20 billion mark sometime between 2025 and 2027. These goals are proof of the position Silicon Europe has achieved. And they reflect its long journey, from the dreams of Italian and French pioneers, to the difficulty in launching the semiconductor industries in these two countries, to the gambles Pistorio took, to the more recent challenges met by Bozotti and Chery with success.

But simply evaluating what awaits ST would be reductive. Chery, one of the sector's top international experts, is the right person to shed some light on the future of the entire semiconductor industry, as well as the geopolitical implications of the current circumstances. The globalization crisis, and the new scenarios arising from the Russian invasion of Ukraine and subsequent economic sanctions: In light of all this, there is an urgent need to rethink the production model used over the previous decades by many major players in the sector. Entrusting Taiwan and other Asian hubs with more than 50 percent of chip production is no longer seen as a wise choice in Brussels and in Washington for a strategic industry like semiconductors. This has set a process in motion that will lead to opening many new fabs in the USA and Europe, and redistributing production in ecosystems with connections to Silicon Valley and Silicon Europe.

It is a historic shift in many ways, and the perfect place to analyze it is in an office in Geneva, where pride of place is taken up by a gigantic poster of a soccer team lined up in a defensive barrier with a one-word caption: Courage. The poster dominates Chery's office and betrays his great passion for soccer, which he constantly uses as a metaphor for the team spirit he asks of his collaborators.

Born in Orléans in 1960 and currently living in Geneva, Chery considers Aix-en-Provence his true home (he is also an Olympique fan) and Paris the place where he got his education. He earned his engineering degree at ENSAM, the French engineering institute of higher education. Then he embarked on his professional career at Matra, and later joined Thomson in 1986, just prior to the merger with the Italians at SGS.

> "I started off in the Tours plant, in the Discrete Division, and I was responsible for customer relations," Chery recollects. "On my second day of work, I met my boss and he asked me: 'Are you the new engineer?' 'Yes.' 'You made a big mistake; this plant is about to close.'
> "That experience stuck with me, because from the outset I always worried about the customers I had to take care of, and at the same time I was afraid they would close the factory on me. I never got over that, and in some sense, I've carried it with me all of my professional life."

In the end, Tours didn't close, but it was repurposed, and right after that Thomson joined the Italian-French joint-venture. Chery advanced quickly along his career path in the group, and at 32 he was already answering directly to Pistorio as head of the supply chain. He ran the production facilities of Tours and Rousset; he lived many years in Asia where he led the group's front-end manufacturing activities; he later became chief technology officer of ST.

Bozotti, who was President and CEO at the time, gave Chery more responsibilities, tasking him first with quality control and then with the digital sector. At that time, in 2013, Chery tried to let his boss know that all these duties might be a little too much.

> "Carlo's response surprised me," Chery recalls. "He told me that if I was interested and if we worked well together, he would groom me to be his successor. It was a gentleman's agreement, based on a clear understanding: I told him that if it happened, great; but if it didn't, the reason would be that we failed to reach our objectives. And we couldn't afford to let that happen, whatever my future prospects might be."

Chery was appointed Chief Operating Officer and later Deputy CEO, heading up all operating activities on the technology side and in production, as well as sales and marketing. It was a difficult period that lasted until 2016, as we've seen.[1] But it passed, and ST had another in-house torch-passing moment two years later, as with Pistorio and Bozotti.

The succession also brought with it a leadership style that was inevitably different, which is natural when top managers come from different cultures and educational backgrounds, "even if the objectives are the same." Bozotti and Chery are two soccer fans who found themselves playing important roles as coaches during their careers. But although Bozotti has a fiery, somewhat aggressive style, like a Mourinho or an Alessandro Conte, Chery bears more resemblance to an even-tempered, pro-Europe Carlo Ancelotti, the only coach in history to win a championship in all five major European soccer tournaments – without letting it go to his head.

> "Carlo [Bozotti] is a very compassionate person, but after a defeat, he would read us the riot act, no holds barred, to shake us up and get a reaction," Chery recollects. "It was probably the right approach when times were really tough, like from 2008 to 2013, when we left the flash memory and application processor businesses. I handle defeats differently. When I had to delay a much-anticipated announcement to the market because we weren't ready, it was a difficult decision with a steep cost, but I took it along with the team; we were all in it together. If we lose a match, the way I see it, we always get back up and move on together, setting our sights on the next victory, and not looking back at the loss."

Team spirit and a "calm in the eye of the storm" approach that Chery probably learned from his family life, raising three daughters.

The lion, the tiger, and the cow

> "My way of seeing things is based very much on the ability to survive and adapt to the circumstances," explains Chery. "Between a pandemic and a war, these years have tested this outlook. It's like walking into an

---

[1] See Chapter 11.

arena without knowing which animal you'll face, whether it's a lion, a tiger or a cow. If you find out there's a lion or a tiger, you had to prepare yourself for a fight. If there's a cow, you have to learn to milk it. I organize my team based on these assumptions: adapt and deal with the situation."

The scenario that Chery foresees in the coming years, as he attempts to hit the $20 billion mark with ST revenues, is characterized mainly

"by three megatrends: the push towards more smart mobility, increased efficiency in managing power and energy, and the widespread dissemination of cloud-connected autonomous things. One of the most impactful transformation megatrends will be electrification, linked to the absolute necessity to decarbonize industry and mobility. The world will produce an increasing number of electric cars, and there will be massive investments in infrastructure that will require more electronics and more semiconductors. Our industry is an essential enabler for these types of processes, and we want to play a decisive role in helping our clients respect emissions reduction goals."

ST is betting big on smart mobility and the industrial sector. But the company isn't overlooking digital infrastructures and the continuous growth in personal electronics, linked to smartphones, accessories, and the escalation that virtual and augmented reality will set in motion with the advent of the metaverse. The automotive sector in turn will be driven by electrification and digitization, with semiconductors playing an even more prominent role than they do today. But major changes are also expected in fields less visible to the general public that are, once again, enabled by semiconductors. Examples are process automation in manufacturing, digitization of factories and energy efficiency solutions.

All of this will inevitably redraw the map of the industry where ST operates too.

"Over the last 30 or 40 years, the semiconductor industry took on a very particular structure," Chery explains. "There is the computer and processor sector, the memory sector, communications, and finally what we can call diversification. Then there are the various subcategories for each one of those, from microprocessors to systems on chip, from sensors to embedded processing solutions on microcontrollers. This has gradually led the industry to come under the control of a few big players: 85 percent of the semiconductor market is controlled by companies that have a market value between $15 or $20 billion and $40 billion. Roughly speaking, we're talking about three companies in the computer industry, maybe seven in communications, four for memories, and around ten in diversification.

"The other major phenomenon which has occurred over this 20-year evolution in the industry," Chery continues, "is the change in business models. In the field of communications devices, the fabless model dominated, with most production relocated to Taiwan, where the largest foundry in the world – TSMC – is based. In the field of computer chips, the model is mixed, with some companies outsourcing production, and others like Intel that take an integrated approach and control the entire value chain. Memory producers, on the other hand, are completely integrated because the added value in that area is the manufacturing process itself. In other words, you don't have to design any software or hardware. Finally, in the field of diversification there is a mix too. Added to this are the suppliers in the value chain. All this to say that the semiconductor industry is a perfect example of globalization, creating strong specializations all over the world, investing a great deal in innovation, and optimizing processes."

Now that we've entered a phase in which globalization is stalling, it will take time to strike a new balance. The financial models developed over the previous decades for the semiconductor industry are also being seriously reconsidered. Open to debate are the choices made by the companies that bet everything on investments in innovative products, and then rewarded their shareholders with substantial dividends. But doing this meant relocating many production activities and much technological research to Asia, in particular partnering with TSMC in Taiwan. Yet even the companies that have integrated the entire value chain (companies such as ST) must factor in the growing complexity linked to moving goods around the globe.

Globalization has maintained its equilibrium for decades, but that now looks precarious. What's more, two years of pandemic followed by war have sent tremors through the world of semiconductors like we've never seen before. In 2022, the US Congress approved the Chips for America Act with rare bipartisan support. In addition, the big chip consumers such as Apple, Microsoft, Google, and Amazon have joined forces with producers such as Intel, IBM, and Qualcomm to form a new lobby, the Semiconductors in America Coalition. Meanwhile Intel announced $20 billion in investments to build new plants in the US (to lessen dependence on Taiwan) and the White House put $39 billion in direct incentives on the table, funds earmarked for semiconductor production, and $13 billion in financing for research. In mid-2023, thanks to the Chips Act, 50 new projects initiated in the US, with private investments totaling $210 billion and the potential to create 44,000 new jobs.

For Europe, too, it's time to play catch up. Silicon Europe wants to increase its share of global production capacity from 10 percent to 20 percent by 2030. It has also finalized its own European Chips Act, which went into effect in September 2023 throughout the EU. The initiative will mobilize €43 billion in investments.[2]

Bonds bridging the two shores of the Atlantic are building. In view of the strategic value of chips, Washington and Brussels are beginning to see initiatives to increase chip production in the US and Europe through the lens of a more coordinated approach. At the same time, China is picking up speed to close the technological gap on the semiconductor front. According to estimates, by 2025, in a decade's time it will have invested $150 billion in initiatives in this field. Japan has also announced $8 billion of public investments in its chip industry, while South Korea will support domestic companies with fiscal incentives totaling $450 billion through 2030.

In this chaotic scenario, the approach ST is following, led first by Bozotti and now Chery, is to be true to its identity, and to respect its history and all its accomplishments from the 1960s till today. The aim is to build a solid Silicon Europe bestriding the Alps with a prominent global presence, and the ability to successfully meet the challenges arising in one of the most complex markets in the world. "Our ambition is to top $20 billion while keeping the operating model we have today, with 75 percent of production done internally and

---

[2] *A Chips Act for Europe,* communication issued by the European Commission, Brussels, February 8, 2022, p. 2.

25 percent outsourced," Chery states. "To accomplish this, we need to boost our production capacity in 300mm wafers, in silicon carbide and in gallium nitride." ST won't discard the competencies accumulated over the years beyond Europe's border either, for example the vertical integration of silicon carbide, centered in Catania, or another front-end production site in Singapore, or assembly and testing facilities in Shenzhen, China, and in Bouskoura, Morocco. Gallium nitride production in Tours will also be integrated, with a portion outsourced to TSMC in Taiwan.

In Crolles, production is being upgraded for 300mm (12 inch) wafers, the true growth accelerator for the semiconductor industry. Crolles has been operational since the 1990s, after the merger, and maintains its status as a driving force of Silicon Europe. And recently the facility has entered a new technological phase in which operations will be increasingly synched with Agrate, with a "digital twins" approach. An agreement signed in June 2023 between ST and Global Foundries paved the way to realizing a new plant for 300mm wafers that will be jointly operated by the two companies. This €7.5 billion project, approved by the European Commission, will be realized with substantial financial support from the French government, within the context of the "France 2030" development plan.

The historic plant on the outskirts of Milan, in the meantime, as of 2022, is home to the brand new 300mm production center. This is one of the standout strategic achievements of the Bozotti–Chery era. "With Carlo, we started working on this project back in the complicated years of his tenure as chief executive, when we still had to shake off the negative fallout of Nokia and other contingencies from that time," Chery recalls. "The idea was originally to set up a pilot plant, but as time went on, we came up with a new strategy that involved building a completely new factory."

In the silicon citadel founded by Floriani and Olivetti, a highly automated factory has emerged, one based on typical "Industry 4.0" production technologies. In the 245,000 square meters of the ST campus in Agrate, a new complex spanning 65,000 square meters has been built, home to a latest-generation, 15,000-square-meter, 300mm clean room. In 2026, when the plant will be running at full capacity, it will turn out a weekly production of 300mm wafers equaling 8,000 units, giving the company enormous growth potential in the smart power sector. Products will mainly go to supply the automotive industry, smart technologies (embedded digital), and personal electronics (consumer analog). Innovation at the facility also encompasses energy efficiency, and boasts carbon neutral refrigeration systems, water recycling, and solutions that align with ST's commitment to achieve total carbon neutrality by 2027.

Investments in this project amount to $3 billion, and the campus will host process engineers, researchers, production and equipment technicians, and production workers – a total of 600 direct jobs, and three times as many indirect jobs, according to company estimates for this type of project.

Catania will also expand its capacity, in this case in silicon carbide, but the most spectacular growth there will be vertical. ST has decided to take a historical step forward and actually start producing the most precious substrates – in silicon carbide – in the town where the adventure of SiC started in the 1990s. A brand new plant is also taking off that will create wafers from powder.

New frontiers

These hubs reflect the synthesis of where Silicon Europe has come from, after decades of complex challenges and adventures, and where it wants to go. For all these plants, a shared future focus is the automotive industry.

"In the car of the future we'll see two types of transformations," Chery explains. "The first pertains to the engine, where we'll move from combustion engines to batteries (and hydrogen too). It will be an enormous transformation in terms of infrastructure, recharging systems, and new players coming onto the market. A massive electrification of all our mobility. At the same time, we'll see more and more digitization emerge, driven by three factors: safety, changes in the car's architecture, and software, and differentiation. This last field ties into the emotional side of the driving experience. Car makers will increasingly become distributors of infotainment services. In the future, our cars will let us enjoy amazing virtual and augmented reality experiences."

Obviously for these areas – new power units and the myriad services we can access while we're driving (or while we're not driving: see self-driving cars) – thousands more semiconductors will be needed, in addition to the ones that are already embedded in all the processes that are activated in our cars. And these sites will be the new homes to the chips that will be an integral part of our urban mobility.

What's more, at Crolles, building on all the experience gained in imaging, this technology will be further refined, with a special focus on facial recognition. Together with cars, smartphones will be fertile ground for innovation in the coming years (and all the devices in their ecosystem such as smart watches and glasses). One field that ST has opted out of is traditional image sensors for the cameras in smartphones. The reason is that for many years the Japanese, especially Sony, have been developing the most advanced technologies in this area. When we turn our phone cameras to focus on the outside world, they let us capture masses of pictures and videos that often end up on social networks. But when we turn them in the other direction, toward ourselves, there's a universe of services such as Face ID by Apple and similar apps by other mobile phone producers that have seen tremendous growth. And what makes them tick are extremely complex technologies that have been under development since the 1970s at LETI, in France. Today, this is what gives Crolles and Silicon Europe the competitive edge.

But semiconductors will take us much farther than any road can, farther still than our experiences with smartphones and metaverses. Indeed, the real frontier is space, especially now that private businesses with their futuristic projects have joined the efforts of government agencies. Such is the case of Elon Musk's SpaceX, a company that ST is collaborating with, and which has become the chief private partner of NASA and the leading contender in the new space race.

There are many more chapters to be written on the history of silicon, and they may mostly tell of space adventures and new frontiers to explore. Semiconductors have already been to space, on probes and satellites, and it just may happen that a piece of Silicon Europe will accompany the first women and men to land on Mars.